An Integrated Boyhood

VOICES OF DIVERSITY
JOHN J. GRABOWSKI, EDITOR

You Can't Be Mexican: You Talk Just Like Me
FRANK S. MENDEZ

My Father Spoke Finglish at Work: Finnish Americans in Northeast Ohio
EDITED BY NOREEN SIPPOLA FAIRBURN

Remembering: Cleveland's Jewish Voices
EDITED BY SALLY H. WERTHEIM AND ALAN D. BENNETT FROM
DOCUMENTS SELECTED BY JUDAH RUBINSTEIN

An Integrated Boyhood: Coming of Age in White Cleveland
PHILLIP M. RICHARDS

An Integrated Boyhood

Coming of Age in White Cleveland

Phillip M. Richards

The Kent State University Press

KENT, OHIO

For the Memory of Clarence and Juanita Richards

Portions of chapter 4 appeared originally in *Cleveland Magazine* and appear with the permission of *Cleveland Magazine*. Portions of chapters 6 and 7 appeared originally in *The Carolina Quarterly*. Portions of chapter 9 appeared originally in *Commentary* and appear with the permission of *Commentary*.

Cataloging information for this title is available at the Library of Congress.

16 15 14 13 12   5 4 3 2 1

Contents

Series Editor's Foreword

JOHN J. GRABOWSKI

An Integrated Boyhood: Coming of Age in White Cleveland by Phillip Richards provides us with an intimate personal view of an era which challenged the expected and accepted in the United States. Richards came of age in Cleveland during the 1960s, a place and period that have now, arguably, become part of the historical canon. Cleveland, as depicted in the canon, is the polyglot declining industrial city which elected Carl Stokes as the first black mayor of a major American city. That regional event is an critical component of the larger 1960s canon, one which contemporary students read as a series of broadly sketched movements and events including the Vietnam War, Civil Rights, Women's Liberation; urban unrest, assassinations, and student rebellion, all of which, some fifty years later, have become increasingly colored by an aura of psychedelic nostalgia and some of which have unfortunately morphed into broad cultural cliches.

Increasingly lost in this lengthening temporal perspective are two seminal and closely related aspects of the 1960s: the search for personal identity and the rediscovery of a national diversity. Many of the movements that characterized the 1960s both derived from and encouraged a personal search for identity, one often linked to sex, color, ethnicity, and issues of individual freedom and choice. Those personal quests led to a rediscovery of the diversity of the United States, something which countered a long held view of America as a melting pot in which old identities melded into a new and all encompassing national identity. Whether personal or communal, these processes were freighted with angst and joy, and were and remain matters of perplexing complexity which resonate today. The series, Voices of Diversity, in which this title has been published, is, in itself, a consequence of that seminal change some five decades ago.

An Integrated Boyhood: Coming of Age in White Cleveland, is an important addition to the series because it so ably reminds us of the "personal" 1960s and the manner in which the changes which took place in that era both derived from and altered the view of self. The memoir does so by taking us to what could be considered the key component of the era, and, indeed, one of the defining characteristics of the American experience over time, race. Richards grew up in the Mt. Pleasant neighborhood of Cleveland, a place of middle-class aspiration and one of the few sections of the city which was somewhat integrated. But while many of Richards' white neighbors and schoolmates may have seen him only in color, he, and particularly his family, saw themselves as a particular shade—aspirational middle class—within that color. It was a status and style that could be viscerally measured against the deportment and "style" of some of the family's relatives whose central city origins denoted another kind of blackness.

This core issue of personal identity was compounded by Richards' integrated adolescence, during which he sensed that even middle-class African Americans would not be fully accepted into the white ethnic world of Cleveland with which he interacted on a daily basis in the classroom, or considered as partners in political power by an entrenched ethnic political machine. But as Richards struggled to find himself, he continued to move further away from the normal and expected and became a participant in key aspects of a decade of change. A gifted student, he gained a scholarship to a privileged, largely white, private day school, and then admittance to Yale. He became enmeshed in the left liberal politics of the period, fell in love with folk songs and someone who sang folk-songs, and throughout this journey through adolescence and young adulthood he found himself continually challenged to measure his changing self against the demands of black solidarity and white acceptance.

The intimacy of Phillip Richards' memoir makes it a powerful agent for moving beyond the clichéd characteristics of one of the most significant eras in American history by placing major change in personal perspective and his voice, in the pages that follow, gives measure to the joys and difficulties of understanding and accepting diversity.

JOHN J. GRABOWSKI, PH.D.
Krieger Mueller Associate Professor of Applied History
Case Western Reserve University
Historian, Vice President for Collections
The Western Reserve Historical Society

CHAPTER ONE

A Hopeful Beginning

On the armoire in our dining room sit two of my parents' wedding pictures. One depicts my mother's family arranged in a semicircle around her elderly mother—a small, wizened dark woman in a white dress; the eldest sister of the family, already careworn, but smiling and holding her mother by the arm; and my mother, radiant in her bridal dress, looking straight ahead. My mother is virginal in a white dress, and covering her face is the traditional wedding veil. Her long black hair falls down her in waves. Beside her is my father. My father is a handsome brown-skinned man of medium height with a meticulously groomed moustache. He wears a double-breasted white tuxedo jacket, a formal shirt, a dark pin-dotted tie, and dark pants. Her clothes and abundant hair exude the traditional qualities and inexperience we associate with the bride. His clothing and trimmed features reflect that he has had an opportunity to acquire personal taste in the real world. They stand facing the camera and even now I recognize their broad grins, subdued beneficence, and begrudging approval. Close inspection, however, reveals that the picture is incomplete: there is only one other man here. He, standing within the circle's arc, is clearly a brother. And he will die shortly after the wedding. There is no father to stand with my grandmother in this picture. The family's patriarch, Jimmie Williams, whose name they retain, died eighteen years before. My mother was raised in the home of her eldest sister, Lee Ella, who took her in, as well as their mother and the second-youngest sister, Gladys. In the process, Lee Ella, already burdened with four children and a ne'er-do-well insurance agent for a husband, has sacrificed herself for the sake of the youngest and oldest members of her family. This sacrifice is, in 1947, after seventeen years, written in her face. This family is placing its hopes for its youngest, most beautiful daughter in the meticulously dressed man standing beside her in the picture.

My mother's family has, under great hardship, done its best for her. The second picture shows her and my father cutting a slice of the wedding cake, their hands clasped together around the knife. She will, the picture asserts, now make a life for herself together with him. It is hard to see from the picture who guides the knife, but their marriage will be like that. As my father will say long after her death—at a youthful sixty-four—one would push, and the other would pull. It did not matter who at any time was doing what.

He, this picture suggests, is the mature man missing from the first portrait of the familial world headed by Lee Ella. She, the second photograph announces, is the object of a masculine desire shaped by experience. For all of the picture's erotic poignancy, it remains in the bounds of not only good but traditional tastes. One of my mother's German refugee teachers at Hampton, remembering the quotation from Freud, might have looked at the picture and recalled what he called the prerequisites for a good life: *arbeiten und lieben,* "work and love." The two are setting off for a life together already equipped with the most basic elements for human happiness.

They have by this time in their young lives together decided to move to Cleveland, drawn by the city's reputation for plentiful good jobs, spacious housing, and large green lawns. They believe that all this will be available to them if they are willing to work hard enough. Their dress and posture betoken—in their slight but noticeable formality—an aspiration to something beyond the material ease implicit in the silk dresses and elegant suit. My parents, however, have gotten it all wrong. In Cleveland, they will scramble for work often beneath their level of education. They will face equal difficulties acquiring a mortgage from city banks, which are still unwilling to lend to middle-class blacks. And they will move from neighborhood to neighborhood in search of the good schools for which the city is known among their educated acquaintances. Cleveland's expanding black ghetto will cast a shadow over any aspiration to culture evident in their wedding photo.

Although this memoir concerns a young life of mistakes, it will not concentrate on theirs. The trail of errors that I trace here from my entrance to elementary school at Robert Fulton in Cleveland's Mount Pleasant neighborhood to my graduation from Yale is my own. My parents and other elders—all appearances to the contrary—bear no responsibility for these errors. Would that I had understood what they explained to me. The uncovering of these faults was the beginning of my conscious life. To be sure, the errors I describe typified the dislocated lives of many middle-class blacks in the segregated Cleveland of the fifties, sixties, and early seventies. I grew up in an era of changing certainties of politics, society, and culture. The faults, however, were my own.

I was born in 1950 in Cleveland, Ohio, where my father had come in 1947 to work in the steel mills and auto factories after World War II. My mother joined him in 1948 after graduating from college, taking up residence at the Colored YMCA founded at the century's beginning to aid black migrants from the South.

Before coming to Cleveland, my parents lived in Hampton, Virginia, where they both experienced an upturn in their fortunes. My father had come to Virginia from Kentucky after failing out of Kentucky State College (now Kentucky State University) and returning to his home in Winchester, Kentucky, only to leave again to attend trade school at Hampton Institute. During the war he sailed on the huge naval aircraft carriers on their shakedown cruises amid German submarines in Chesapeake Bay. It was in Hampton that he met my mother. Although he did not finish trade school, his marriage constituted newly solid footing in the world. He made the trip to Cleveland hopeful that his fortunes in the postwar industrial North would continue to improve.

My mother's stay in Hampton also ended in success. She had come to Hampton Institute from Greensboro, North Carolina, where she was raised by her eldest sister, Lee Ella Cheek, after the death of their father. She excelled in her studies and graduated with honors from Hampton, declining a fellowship to Bank Street College of Education at Columbia University. She talked to me often about her early life, and as a child I came to understand why she abandoned an academic career for marriage and a family. A pre-med scholarship student, she had not had much of a social life during college. Her union with my father provided her with new emotional stability and support. She married to acquire what her sisters described as the stable family life that they lost when their father died in 1929, when she was four. She knew of this comfortable family life only from hearsay.

Many blacks drawn by Cleveland's promise had come to the city in migratory waves in the first fifty years of the twentieth century. Like the late nineteenth-century black writer Charles Chesnutt—also a quondam North Carolina inhabitant—they found the city's thriving business district, factories, and tree-lined neighborhoods a sign of hope. Although my parents found it difficult being so isolated from their tightly knit, geographically close families, there was consolation. They had known rural Kentucky and coastal Virginia amid the strains of Depression-era poverty and the trauma of World War II mobilization. Despite Cleveland's strangeness, they experienced in their new home a deep exhilaration that they would remember for the rest of their lives. Other events in 1948, the first year of their married life in the city, seemed to justify their dreams. They were fond of reminding themselves that a number of Cleveland's professional sports teams had won league titles that year, and that Cleveland was briefly nicknamed "the city of champions."

My parents' happiness was primarily due to their rapid acquisition of domestic comfort in a city with scarce housing for middle-class blacks. After two years in their first home together, a tiny kitchenette in Glenville, they moved to Mount Pleasant, where they purchased a two-story brown-shingled bungalow on tree-lined 137th Street. They stretched themselves to the last penny to do this, applying to one of the city's established wealthy Negroes for a loan to make their down payment. Two friends from Phillis Wheatley rented the house's paste-walled attic to help with the mortgage. For a long time, my mother worked as a teacher at Park Synagogue in Cleveland Heights. As my father gained seniority as a custodian for the Cleveland Board of Education, his income increased and the mortgage became less burdensome, allowing the boarders to leave before I was old enough to remember them.

At five and six years old, my sister Patrice and I found my parents' continuing excitement remarkable and a little embarrassing. We had never known anything other than our Mount Pleasant house, whose gray sofa, thin rug, and spartan kitchen seemed plain and unexceptional compared to the brightly colored carpets, lounge chairs, and dining-room outfits of our aunt and friends' families. We watched with amazement as Mom and Dad enthused over every aspect of the coffee tables, bedroom sets, and piano that they had purchased with their savings from the previous few years. We could not understand the pride they exuded on Saturday mornings when they served waffles at our modest vinyl-covered breakfast table.

By any measure, Clarence and Juanita experienced ample success compared to their fellow migrants. However, they could not ignore the racially grounded social, economic, and political realities that had already set limits on their aspirations by the late fifties. When we children were presumed to be out of hearing range, my parents discussed the obstacles to their economic progress that they faced. These included my father's difficulties obtaining steady decent work despite some college and trade school education, as well as the banks' obvious restrictions on housing loans to middle-class blacks, difficulties that had been faced by black newcomers to Cleveland throughout the century, and which, beginning in the twenties, were complicated by the presence of European "ethnics," which included not only the well-entrenched Germans but recently arrived southern and eastern Europeans. The WASP elite favored this population as factory workers, and black workers experienced increased opportunities only during wartime shortages.

Their troubles were exacerbated by the shifting ethnic boundaries within the city. My parents arrived in Glenville at a time when these areas were still relatively integrated; however, these neighborhoods were quickly transformed into black ghettoes. The bars, crowded barber shops, groups of unemployed men on corners, hustlers, numbers runners, pimps, and teenage gang members inevitably took the underclass culture—along with the blues, religious ritual, and folk talk—wherever Cleveland's black world expanded. This occurred quickly in Mount Pleasant in the fifties, although its overwhelmingly white population had been sprinkled with a few blacks since the beginning of the twentieth century. My family's movement from Mount Pleasant to Invermere in Lee-Harvard, to the Severn Road neighborhood off Taylor Road, and eventually to Forest Hills in the upper Monticello portion of East Cleveland would—to my mother's dismay—mirror the city's internal migration of middle- and upper-middle-class blacks.

My parents responded to the expansion of Cleveland's ghetto culture with distress bordering on hysteria. Already in the late fifties my parents began to express their horror at the dispersal of Cleveland's ghetto population to Mount Pleasant as the Negroes of Hough, Glenwood, and Collinwood, whom my parents had escaped in the late forties, began to appear in our own neighborhood. As my mother and I walked home from the 140th Street library on Friday afternoons, she would discern the telling signs of this inner-city migration: storefront Baptist churches; bars such as the Flame on Kinsman, whose open doors breathed the thick odor of gin; and slick numbers runners and pimps prowling the streets in flashy suits of electric blue or green. Through the plate-glass windows of the barbershop farther east on Kinsman, we could see men idling on padded metal chairs, epitomizing the unruly indirection of inner-city life.

During the course of my boyhood, my parents persistently struggled to buy homes in better and better neighborhoods, going from bank to bank in search of loans, often reaching the point of closing only to have the deal fall through. On Sundays, we often toured suburban areas by car. Our parents, we gradually realized, were preparing an escape not only from the lower-class Negro masses but from blacks in general. My parents found, however, to paraphrase Joe Louis, the great black proletarian hero of the forties, that they could run but they could not hide.

Before I ever heard the word, I knew that my parents were integrationists. They were what Malcolm X would later derisively call "integration-mad Negroes." Struck by the recent triumphs of Jackie Robinson, Ralph Bunche, and *Brown v. Board of Education,* they imagined the imminent appearance of a cultivated, racially integrated middle-class life in Cleveland. These utopian hopes could not have been more mistaken. The possibility of a racially integrated existence had disappeared long ago with the cultivated, mulatto, elite culture that had existed during the first half of the nineteenth century. These black middle-class tradesmen, artisans, funeral directors, barbers, and entrepreneurs had lived relatively harmoniously with Cleveland whites before the turn of the century. The writer Charles Chesnutt, a highly successful lawyer as well as a man of letters, was an important part of this elite. Chesnutt sent one of his daughters to Smith, another to Flora Stone Mather College at Western Reserve University (now Case Western Reserve University), and a son to Harvard. He was a member of the city's major literary, social, and cultural organizations. He would write not only collections of stories but a series of novels concerning the post-Reconstruction South and the new world of the black urban North, and in the teens and twenties, he would bitterly attack the new racism that accompanied Negro migration to the city. As the ghetto formed, the city's mulatto community disappeared by attrition; and its descendents intermarried with the dark-skinned newcomers from the South. All but a few found themselves absorbed into the world of the southern arrivals, which included not only an unskilled proletariat but also an aspiring professional middle class. Rejected by whites and isolated in the ghetto, the black migrants from the South quickly formed their own institutions.

Except for a few remarkable individuals with whom my parents had no actual contact, their cultural ambitions had no accessible black models. Looking around them, my parents could see examples of their ideal only in figures such as Zelma George, the actress and singer, and the artists and writers of Cleveland's Karamu House, an interracial center for theater and high culture. This posed an insoluble problem for them and, as they saw it, a barrier to the successful rearing of their children.

Moving from Glenville to Mount Pleasant, my parents continued in the habits of typical southern migrants of their generation. They, like many of our black neighbors, gardened vigorously every summer, in late August canning our garden's yield of tomatoes, bright yellow squash, and green beans grown on high poles. From our backyard border fence they gathered thick-skinned concord grapes. They also canned peaches, pears, and apples purchased from the farmers' market across the Cuyahoga River in the Near West Side—an apparently racially neutral commercial area, at least on Saturdays. They attended Antioch Baptist Church regularly, teaching Sunday school and going to the noonday sermon while we children participated in junior church run by the minister's wife. They also read the well-established black newspaper the *Call and Post,* edited by the Republican William O. Walker, following the fortunes of black politicians and the paper's attacks on segregation in Cleveland.

However, my parents never completely belonged to those black cultural institutions whose deepest values they would seem to have shared. At times, they blamed their estrangement on their cultural and social habits: they did not drink, smoke, curse, or frequent the jazz joints downtown. Not until the seventies and eighties did they begin to attend events of the Hampton Institute alumni group. Some of the alumni, such as the opera singer Grace Mims and her husband Howard, who would become a professor at Cleveland State, were already distinguished. However, they seemed to know that illustrious couple only by name and reputation.

My parents rejected the alumni as snobs, often citing as an example a pompous dentist who openly attacked members incapable of making large contributions. Despite the political consciousness of the *Call and Post,* they mocked the pretensions of the blacks in its society pages, called it sensationalistic, and contemptuously rejected the pragmatic Republican politics of its editor, who had had no other political choices during the thirties, forties, and fifties. At the same time, they eschewed the urbanized black proletariat from the South surrounding us. Their straight-laced habits made them homeless among Cleveland's freewheeling black world. Although they would appear to be aspiring to the highest sphere of black Cleveland life, one assumes that they might judge the drinking, talk, gambling, and frequenting of jazz clubs there at least as harshly as anything they had found in proletarian life. My mother and father kept to themselves, tended to the rearing of their children, and forbade us—me and my sisters—to immerse ourselves in the declining black world around us. In their own way, they walled the family off from our immediate community. They drew, I suspect, much of their ambitions for their children's education from a fire that fed on resentment acquired before I knew them.

My siblings and I, however, took for granted the cultural activities in which our parents immersed us. As they would often remind us over dinner, they pinched pennies to put us in what they called "good situations," a string of high-minded activities intended to prepare us for a racially integrated world of culture. These included music theory and piano lessons at the Cleveland settlement house and then the Cleveland Institute of Music as well as Dalcroze classes and reading programs at the public library on 140th and Kinsman in Mount Pleasant. This aspiration to culture, we soon realized, explained the rigor of our summer vacations, which included day camp run by a local civic organization, and later Hiram House overnight camp for two weeks, as well as eight-week sessions of French lessons at the Western Reserve University demonstration school for new language teachers. Our parents assumed that these activities would allow us as a family to transcend Cleveland's ghetto world, the reality of the black community on the East Side, which was dominated by a transplanted and urbanized southern black proletarian religious, political, and social ethos of the bars, storefront churches, and crowded allies of the Hough, Central, and Glenville slums.

Our upbringing was also characterized by an asceticism opposed to the "extravagant" and "flamboyant" manner shared, according to my parents, by the black elite and the masses. My parents sought to teach us to resist not only the ghetto ethos but the ostentatious snobbery that they attributed to upper-class blacks. Similarly, they conceived of their rigorous saving and frugal habits of dress, eating, and entertainment—we watched TV only briefly on weekends under our parents' supervision—as a means of distinguishing ourselves from these styles of the ghetto.

For them, the ghetto was not a demographic abstraction but a symbol of the pathology of blackness itself—a pathology to be resisted by stringently budgeted daily lives. Only their economies, my parents felt, kept them suspended over the ghetto abyss into which they might fall. This high-wire act carried its own psychology of building internal pressures not unlike the dangers posed by the steam boilers my father attended to as a custodian at A. J. Rickoff or Robert Fulton Elementary School. Like an untended boiler, these pressures threatened internal damage and eventual explosion.

My earliest memories of this domestic anxiety depict my parents poring over the bills on Friday night and Saturday morning, the culmination of a week of worry. The financial stocktaking on Friday evenings and Saturday mornings measured the toll of the week's expenditures in the writing of checks and the recording of bank balances. Seemingly endless sums were calculated and often recalculated in my mother's looping handwriting on long white business envelopes. The clearing of these proliferating columns from the table signaled the household's true measure of time: the end of a week's bookkeeping.

All the advantages that we enjoyed, my older sister and I were given to understand, hung in a balance with the tiny fund that provided us with ground meat and soup bones, tomatoes, lettuce, and carrots, as well as toothpaste, soap, and shampoo. This penury was alleviated only by coupons clipped from the previous week's morning newspaper supplements and the Sunday advertisement section.

Restricted to our house and its surrounding yard, I grew up within the compass of my family's inner and outer restraints. Although physically healthy, I was uncoordinated and clumsy. I could not swing a baseball bat or throw a ball properly. This incompetence made me a target of my classmates' teasing, and as a child, I developed a sensitivity that resulted in an explosive but usually hidden temper that revealed itself at the most unexpected moments. Some of this anger took the form of malingering or sabotage. Denied the freedom of the playground, I was disobedient. When my father cleaned the leaves from the gutter with a stream of water during spring housecleaning, I would randomly turn on the spigot to watch the foaming bubbles at my end of the transparent hose. He whipped me for this, but I was always angry enough to do it again at the end of the summer. I was only letting off steam. My older sister behaved even more outrageously. Three or four hours into our regular pilgrimages through Cleveland's old downtown Halle's and Higbee's department stores, we would typically become ravenous with hunger, and then angry when our parents—who we knew carried money for a day's worth of parking at the multilevel concrete city parking lots—refused to buy us hot dogs and peanuts from the vendors tending metal carts along the streets. One hot day, my sister's patience ran out. In outraged desperation, she filched several handfuls of honeyed peanuts and gummy fruits from the open canisters in the confectionary section of May Company. Seeing her with the stolen candy as we prepared to leave the store, my horrified father threatened to turn her in to the police. I profited from his preoccupation with my sister by filling my own pockets with sweets.

Upon returning home, my parents immediately sent Patrice to her bedroom. She was confined there until the family finished dinner. In the car, she had insisted that this punishment meant nothing to her. Still surging with rebellion at home, she gorged herself in her bedroom, she later boasted to me, on the chocolates, nuts, and sugared fruits that she had earlier salted away in her purse. Her defiance persisted when my parents called her down to the living room. Emboldened by her heightened blood sugar, she shouted over the stairway banister that she would steal wherever she pleased then returned to her bedroom, slamming the door shut. My parents stared for a moment at her door and returned to the kitchen to consider further action. She had shocked the entire family. In the wake of this event, the very air circulating through the house still quivered with her rage.

My father's mention of the police in the store was not unusual, although he knew that they would not be bothered by such trivial matters. How could they care about missing candy corn, given the number of black pimps and drunks everywhere on the streets? What would they do but return my sister and me to our parents after such petty thefts? Yet our parents continually warned us against engaging in the displays of disrespect toward the police that we saw practiced by the young black teenagers who called them "cops," mocked their movements, and gathered around the squad cars during the school fights that took place with increasing frequency following afternoon dismissals at Robert Fulton and St. Cecilia. (Our teachers at Robert Fulton Elementary School checked our pockets for sharpened pencils and knives before our dismissal on the days of anticipated fights.)

The police kept an eye out for crime in Cleveland's black community; and our criminal motives, my parents stressed, were implicit in our blackness. Alone on the street, we could not be parsed out from our less polite black fellows. We were continually under their official scrutiny, a powerful extension of the city's white Polish, Hungarian, and Italian authority that could land us in court, a holding pen, or reform school rather than our kitchen, where we would merely be whipped. It was not uncommon to see black youngsters driven away in squad cars after school fights. This, according to our parents, could only be the beginning of judgment by an impersonal white law.

These fears were reinforced by the newspaper headlines of the evening *Press,* the *Call and Post,* and the only slightly more restrained *Cleveland Plain Dealer.* Their front pages and features sections frequently carried stories of the presence, apprehension, trials, imprisonment, and execution of black criminals. In the eyes of the city's media, these black criminals represented Negro rage against Cleveland's eastern European and Italian establishment and tarnished the respectability of the colored population. The black criminals were, in our minds, part of a drama around which our sense of acceptable and unacceptable Negro behavior turned. Barely more acceptable were black lawyers, the defenders of the colored criminals, and sometimes their white mob bosses.

Finally, my parents feared that the horrors of black criminal excess and behavior might penetrate the blood boundaries of our isolated Cleveland family.

My Aunt Gladys and Uncle Lonnie's marriage offered a glimpse of the social collapse threatened by black city existence that my parents so feared. Gladys had come to Cleveland from Newport News shortly after my mother's arrival. She was accompanied by her husband, Lonnie, an army veteran trained as a dental hygienist. (His prospects had made him a more favored prospective in-law than my father for my mother's family.) Educated as a nurse, she had passed her national nursing board examination a year before her expected graduation from North Carolina College for Negroes in Durham. Even though she never graduated from college, she worked as a nurse for her entire professional life and was, by her own account, the first black registered nurse hired in Cleveland's VA hospital. She was an elegant, well-dressed woman whose temperament swung from manic excitement to depression. Sadly, her domestic life was horrific. She was constantly abused by her husband not only emotionally but physically.

Lonnie's intended career as a dental hygienist never materialized, and he soon obtained work with the post office, a stable, relatively generous federal employer that allowed black men to provide their families with middle-class lives. At work he drove a mail truck, making special deliveries. Although he and Gladys earned what my mother called "good money"—certainly more than my parents—Lonnie did not follow this path to bourgeois life. Indeed, he clearly repudiated the family's Puritan morality and their middle-class aspirations. Gladys and Lonnie lived in an apartment on the top floor of a duplex house. His drinking, gambling, and consorting with women interfered with his contribution to the household income, and their spending was too undisciplined to provide adequate credit for the purchase of a home. We would often spend Sunday and weekday afternoons together in their upstairs home. At home Lonnie was seldom sober, although nowhere in their house did I ever see liquor. Indeed, I seldom saw Lonnie for long. After a brief appearance, he eagerly fled our presence, probably for his friends downtown.

Lonnie flouted our standards of respectability in more serious ways. Both my mother and father refrained from openly displaying affection or discussing sexual matters. Although they shared a deep affection, they would exchange only brusque pecks in our presence. So shocking was Lonnie's behavior, however, that my mother broke this strict code in conversation with me. When I was in my early teens, during Gladys's divorce, my mother told me in a hushed, faltering voice that Lonnie had made "indiscreet demands" of my aunt. I did not understand what she meant by this until I was forbidden to wear Lonnie's swimsuit when I forgot to bring my own trunks to a family picnic. My father explained to me that Lonnie hired prostitutes in the Hough and Glenville slums, which raised fears of sexually transmitted diseases. His drinking eventually metastasized into alcoholism, which destroyed his ability to hold any position at the post office or to find a job elsewhere. As his savings from his relatively generous salary dried up, he himself deteriorated. To no one's surprise, his decaying body was discovered in an empty ghetto building sometime in the early sixties. No cause for his death was ever identified.

At nine or ten years of age, I felt an immediate attraction to Lonnie and his defiance. His manner exuded the anger that I felt during piano practice, chores with my father, and forced marches downtown to buy the same blue oxford shirts and khakis time after time. Lonnie's arrogance also reflected my sister's deeper rage, which won her even more strapping from my father—about three a month—than the one or two I received. (I was angry about this and kept careful count.) The rebellious stylishness of black life oozed from Lonnie's leather jackets, Ban-Lon shirts, sharkskin pants, and then-fashionable ribbed silk socks. Similarly attractive to me was the carelessness with which he smoked, his cigarette—usually a Camel—dangling from his lips. He wore sleek sunglasses as much for effect as need. His hair was cut short but tastefully oiled, his moustache fastidiously trimmed. Even dressed in his blue serge post-office uniform, he exuded a sense of confidence.

Lonnie enjoyed saying shocking things, many of which I only gleaned from my parents' conversations after visits with my Aunt Gladys. She had at one time obviously been attracted to Lonnie's raffish manners and enjoyed shocking my mother as well as my father. Even after they separated and divorced, Lonnie continued to be a presence in Gladys's home, and his appearance led to scenes that evoked emotions that my mother and father ordinarily did not display at home. "What has four legs, three eyes, and a white pussy?" Lonnie asked one time at a gathering of friends during the Christmas season, referring to the short, black one-eyed Sammy Davis Jr. and his tall blonde Swedish wife, May Britt. Embarrassed by the use of such language in the presence of children, my mother and father flinched, put down their glasses of eggnog, hustled us into the car, and drove off, my father tight lipped and my mother open mouthed, silent with rage. I rarely heard Lonnie speak for long, but his obscenity assaulted the senses like a punch to the belly. Amid our polite family gatherings, his spiel of curses was almost political—brutalizing, defying, and confronting his surprised middle-class audience with the nihilism of the black ghetto world.

The scene that I recall most vividly, recounted by my parents in whispers, concerned my grandmother, who had come from the South when I was about five to help my parents raise my sister and me. She was a small, slender woman who wore dark floral prints and kept half-dollars rolled in the foot of one of her flesh-colored stockings. She took snuff, which my father bought for her at the drugstore. She had, in the early twentieth century, been the wife of a successful farmer near Weldon, North Carolina, on the Virginia border. After losing her husband and property during the Depression, she had recovered a stable life in the home of my Aunt Lee Ella.

From my grandmother's point of view, Gladys's marriage to this drunkard was a sign of the family's decline into the urban ghetto. My grandmother would glare at Lonnie when she saw him and sometimes would shake her fist at him for no reason. Typically he responded to her fist shaking with only a bland stare. After one intense confrontation, however, he had had enough. Standing up and looking her straight in the face, he unzipped the fly of his post-office pants, withdrew his long brown member, and waved it at her. The horrified old woman was finally silenced, but Lonnie continued to stand there, shaking his genitalia like a fairy-tale godmother's wand, pronouncing a curse on the family matriarch, her clan's pretentions, and their bourgeois absurdity.

CHAPTER TWO

The Ghetto Within

Gladys's marriage to Lonnie embodied the horrors of Cleveland's black world—its rage, drunken violence, and willful destructiveness as well as its style, flamboyance, and excessive spending. Despite my parents' desire to seal off the ghetto from our surroundings, my uncle brought this world into our home. His appearance during Sunday family dinner or at a Saturday picnic announced a truth that the family, despite its efforts, could not deny. No black person, no matter how reclusive, could escape the reality of Cleveland's ghetto culture, however far into Lee-Harvard, Warrensville Heights, Shaker Heights, or East Cleveland he or she might go. If one did not go into the streets to seek it, it would enter one's home, shaking its penis.

Lonnie's lifestyle may well have suggested to my mother that this reality had shaped my father's early solitary stay in Cleveland, when he worked in the city while my mother finished her last year at Hampton Institute. Lonnie represented the urban hell that, according to my mother, almost swallowed my father during his year alone in the city after their wedding. This, however, was to compare great things to small. Coming to Cleveland to find work, Clarence Richards had, by this account, found himself at sea. After working the night shift in the West Side plants, he roamed the still-dark streets near his apartment on 105th Street, going out for rib or fish sandwiches at two or three in the morning. He often ran low on money and found himself borrowing from the next week's payroll. Amid the iron mills and automobile factories, my father drifted, unable to save money or achieve steady employment and the possibility of social advancement. His early life in the city, according to my mother, seemed a fulfillment of any prediction that my mother's relatives would have made on the basis of his earlier life at Kentucky State, Hampton Institute, and the shipyards during the war. Whatever difficulties black men had in the industrial North, my mother's southern cousins and in-laws had parlayed their trades into successful careers in contracting as carpenters or builders. From the perspective of her relatives, my father was a failure.

A less sanguine view might be that my father's dislocation was the result of the disorienting reality of city life that he faced after having never lived anywhere but in tiny rural Winchester, Kentucky, and along the docks of Newport News, Virginia. He had done little besides unsuccessfully attend college in Kentucky and Virginia; sing in a musical quartet, like many black men of his era; and court the pretty girls at Hampton Institute. In Cleveland he confronted a short-age of skilled jobs for blacks and the traumatic conditions facing workers in steel mills and automobile factories. Men lost hands and limbs amid the whir-ring of heavy machinery that rattled his nerves and dried his mouth.

My mother's experience in Cleveland, she told me, was, despite her marital happiness, an exercise in self-sacrifice. She had given up a fellowship at the Bank Street College of Education at Columbia in New York to come to Cleveland. Like other black arrivals from the South, she—as she told me many a time—confronted a vast foreign urban expanse that seemed more like Prague than a midwestern American city. She first worked in sewing shops and factories—sweatshops, really—where she toiled in cramped, airless rooms alongside heavy, sweaty, pushing-and-shoving Polish and Hungarian women. Her explanations for her decision to temporarily abandon work and stay at home hid a deeper reality. Unlike many newly arrived black women of her age from the South, she refused to consider daily or weekly employment as a housekeeper in the wealthy white homes of Cleveland and Shaker Heights. Her familial pride, it may be assumed, would never allow her to become what she must have seen as a servant. Her decision to leave work and remain home and run the household was, paradoxically, the salvation of their finances. With her sharp tongue, she disciplined my father and saved money for their household and family. The rejection of their fellow newcomers to the North was part of this ascetic re-gime. They came to represent Lonnie's waywardness and the city life that had threatened briefly to destroy my father. By the early sixties, only my mother's vehement harangues evinced her antagonism toward these erstwhile friends and their fancy new Buicks, Oldsmobiles, and Cadillacs. Wasted money, my mother liked to say, was always needed later on. Their fellows from the South paid for these luxuries with garnished wages, bad credit, and repossessions. By this time, her ire at the memories of this flamboyant middle-class wastefulness extended to the luxurious lifestyles of the successful black bourgeois snobs who, she claimed, snubbed our family in church, clubs, and social events.

Yet my father must have enjoyed in some sense the freedom on Cleveland's empty streets at night. Years later in the late fifties, driving me along Euclid or Carnegie Avenue in Hough and Glenville, he would point out the shops where he had bought sandwiches late at night or early in the morning after leaving work and returning to his apartment. A picture of his solitary year in Cleveland different from my mother's account of his wayward drifting slowly emerged. In an urban world with little work for black men, he had in the course of moving from job to job—White Motors, Reliance Electric, and the Cleveland Transit System—managed to stay employed. Through the rigors of black city life he had succeeded in rolling with the punches, riding out the rough spots, and always landing on his feet. During the rare times when he bathed me, he told me of losing his job as a mechanic. (He was an excellent car repairman, even more skilled than his auto mechanics teachers at Hampton, who would call upon him to get their vehicles running in the dead of winter.) His lonely walks searching for a job before he landed a position as a fireman (essentially a laborer who shoveled coal into the steam furnaces then in use) with the Cleveland Board of Education constituted the most difficult period of his life. He sensed at that time, he told me in his level, laconic voice, a deep, empty pit in his stomach.

My father, however, made only token challenges to my mother's interpretation of his first year in Cleveland. He understood their differences and showed a willingness to adapt to a new life. He loved my mother and admired her ability to harvest such a bounty from his meager salary with her severe economies. They had married at the end of his drifting youth, when he desired a stable family life. When they met, he was a man with sexual experience and an active social life, and my mother was clearly drawn to the powerful masculinity embodied not only in his freewheeling social manners but also in his strong, sturdy brown frame. They clandestinely took baths together, an erotic ritual my sister Patrice and I discovered by accident when we once came home early from a church party. In a way, my mother reciprocated my father's goodwill. She tolerated the periodic dry cleaning of his clothes, including a silk-banded grey felt fedora—a remarkable luxury for this otherwise parsimonious pair. According to my father, their year apart brought them closer as the two corresponded between Hampton and Cleveland. Growing up, I rarely saw my father write more than the letters of a crossword puzzle. But after finishing our Saturday afternoon chores, we often went to the attic, where he showed me the shoe box holding his correspondence with my mother during that year: a thick bundle of yellowed envelopes bulging against the box's cardboard sides. My parents were powerfully linked, but in a way as eccentric as their personalities and contradictions.

There was no getting around my family's oddness, its refusal to conform to the enjoyments and general understanding of black city life whether in Glenville or Mount Pleasant, whose populations eventually became identical anyway. During breakfast on Saturdays, my parents repeatedly explained to a leery son and daughters exactly who we were, how we'd become that way, and what we were doing. These discussions became a verbal commedia dell'arte of the heroes, rogues, saints, and fools populating my parents' lives at Kentucky State and Hampton and the plants and sweatshops of Cleveland.

During these discussions I learned that my mother had acquired her stern perspective on black life in her sister Lee Ella's striving Greensboro household in a black community dominated by lawyers, doctors, ministers, and professors at the local Negro colleges: Bennett, North Carolina A&T, North Carolina School for Negroes, and Shaw, among others. These people directed visiting professors, ministers, and other luminaries to Lee Ella, who not only boarded them briefly, since decent Southern hotels were then segregated, but prepared their meals and mended their clothes to earn extra money for the household. At the same time, Lee Ella, according to my mother, taught school; did the bookkeeping for her husband, King, a struggling railway agent; and ensured that her sisters led upright moral lives. In Lee Ella's household, my mother encountered learned black men whose example led her to admire the ambitious young black professors at Hampton working on their doctorates during the summer in Chicago or at Columbia, bringing the academic authority of Hyde Park and Morningside Heights back to Greensboro, North Carolina, in the fall. These inclinations also drew her to another group of intellectuals who frequented the black colleges during wartime: the German and eastern European Jewish immigrants, who were limited to teaching in southern black schools.

Even a lonely withdrawn boy could see that my mother's bourgeois bearing was at least partially meant as recompense for the snubs of the upper-class people who surrounded and looked down upon her. She had been an excellent student throughout elementary and secondary school, graduating as salutatorian of her class at Greensboro's Dudley High School. Choosing to go to Hampton out of fear of Howard's intricate social class system—she had been offered a scholarship to the Washington, D.C., school—she nevertheless found herself trapped in a strict social hierarchy at Hampton. Few of her black peers in Greensboro and Hampton could, she must have imagined, legitimately attack her when she surrounded herself with authentic intellectuals. From this perspective, most of her attackers could be dismissed as trifling dilettantes who were, in the language of the black college, "standing, styling, and profiling" and, more important, unsure of their real intellectual merit.

My mother often expressed her resentment in invidious comparisons that she made between black newcomers to the academy and German and eastern European Jewish intellectuals who enjoyed generations of cultivation. Compared to this Continental elite, even the distinguished Davis family seemed arrivistes. The Davises have, since my parents' time, been a formidable presence in the black academic world. Years later at Howard I met Arthur P. Davis, then in retirement, who wrote the first serious scholarly literary criticism of African American literature. His nephew Charles Davis was a Dartmouth graduate and a distinguished editor of Walt Whitman's writing who ended his career as a chaired professor at Yale shortly after I graduated. The family includes in my generation the accomplished opera composer Anthony Davis and the writer-journalist Thulani Davis. But long before I understood the importance of these luminaries, I heard their supercilious family and its arrogant Phi Beta Kappa descendants berated and dismissed by my parents over Saturday morning waffles.

The remarkable accomplishments of this black family and other black intellectuals meant little to my mother. Even as a college student and young adult, she was aware that she was not part of Hampton's genteel nineteenth-century world represented by the Davises. Yet she had nevertheless internalized that elite's residual nineteenth-century Protestant-Victorian values. For her, their accomplishments were overshadowed by her assumption that they would snub a bright light-skinned but poor black woman. At school she was also made painfully aware of class snobbery (sometimes masking itself as color caste snobbery) among her more popular classmates. In graduate school, I acquired a middle-class friend whose aunt had known my mother at Hampton. The two had despised each other. My friend's aunt politely declined to discuss Juanita Richards. My mother, her face reddening at the mention of her name, described the now-elderly woman as "some runaround."

A romantic image of her family's past emerged—one more powerful than any of the realities of her life as a child growing up with her sister, Lee Ella, in Greensboro. This image drove my mother's academic accomplishment, intellectual zeal, and pursuit of culture. From the bits and pieces of her family memories, she had confected a vision of the family's past glory. Central to this vision was a half-white father who built a beautiful white house in Weldon, North Carolina, and gained the respect of both blacks and whites, who came to him for advice not only on hunting and farming but also on political matters. In this dream, her father drove an Essex, then the most prestigious car on the road. His possessions and influence throughout the county made him the most powerful man, black or white, in the community.

In the evening, as my mother watched me rinse myself clean after she had scrubbed my back, she would predict the family's future glory. She explicitly conveyed to me the path that my intellectual development should take. As I wiped the soap from my eyes, she would tell me about how she had graduated from college with a double major in home economics and child development, passing with distinction all the classes required for entrance to medical school. She would speak hopefully of the Major Work program, Cleveland's program for gifted public school students; other elite educational programs around the country, including the University of Chicago's Laboratory School; and the opening of formerly segregated universities such as Brooklyn College, the University of Chicago, and Queens College to blacks. In her dream, an influential black life of the mind would come to exist.

At the heart of this intellectualism was what she called "culture" and "cultivation," which she located not in the southern black schools—where, before desegregation, these things were highly visible—but in prewar Germany and New England, the University of Chicago, and Columbia and Bank Street College. She most admired cultured individuals on the margins of their social worlds: the struggling émigré instructors. Such professors included a refugee professor of home economics from Germany, a disgruntled chemistry instructor who once closed the laboratory door and exhorted his students to flee Hampton. She also admired a Chicago-educated professor of English who taught American literature. When I got to the University of Chicago as a graduate student in English, I looked up her record and found that she had written an important dissertation on folk culture. According to my mother, she was a hard taskmaster who assigned the whole of *Moby-Dick* to the class and spoke to her students of nothing but "Eliot, Eliot, Eliot" in her free time.

This eccentric orientation may have linked her in a complicated way to my father, who had been a hapless sociology student at all-black Kentucky State and afterward at Hampton Institute's trade school. He too was connected to a world of culture, although he presented himself as the son of a poor Kentucky miner ditchdigger. Despite his educational failings, once one began to talk with him, it became clear that he possessed a comprehensive view of black history.

He was, in his own way interested in culture. He saw Langston Hughes perform at Kentucky State in the early thirties and followed Paul Robeson's early career as an actor and singer as well as his tragic experience in radical politics, Charles Chesnutt's life in nineteenth-century Cleveland, the founding of the NAACP, the city's Karamu Theatre (which had produced some of Hughes's drama), and, on the darker side, the fate of Cleveland's political radicals who had participated in the postwar labor movements. He made thoughtful observations on the history, reputation, and importance of these people and offered a view from experience, which she had, for all her academic striving, apparently overlooked.

His world of culture—though deeply informed by classical music—focused on the explosion of black music, theater, and literature in the first half of the century. He was an acute observer of the world who had perceived the rise of Nazism in the Hitler Youth movement as an example of political excess. As a worker in the wartime shipyards during World War II (this occupation exempted him from the draft), he sailed on the "shakedown cruises" of the great aircraft carriers and destroyers, some of which had been destroyed in the attack on Pearl Harbor. At the Hampton docks he saw German soldiers taken from captured U-boats—they sometimes pursued American ships on their trial runs. He witnessed jokes that ended in horrific tragedies: a man clowning around who fell to his death from the height of a destroyer's bridge, and another killed when his partner playfully stuck the hose of an air pump over his accidently exposed anus. His intestines, my father blandly remarked, spewed along the deck. He said this directly, without emphasis. The moral of the story was that the great cultural movements and the politics they inspired easily devolved into devastating human tragedies. He reflected on these events and their racial significance in a thoughtful way that would have attracted my mother, who, as a college student, had little experience of the world beyond Lee Ella's sheltered Greensboro home and the Hampton campus and must have seemed remarkably innocent to him despite her intelligence. The knowledge he shared with her, moreover, probably offered much enlightenment on her earlier life in the South as well as in Cleveland. Both of my parents' racial attitudes were conditioned by the interracial attitudes of Hampton Institute and, I suspect, through my father's mother, who had attended Berea College, in Kentucky. These were worlds where progressive white instructors consorted with blacks. These were also worlds of transplanted New England culture, which valued the Anglo-American literary classics, who had transcribed the spirituals into conventional musical notations, and who cultivated European tastes in symphonies, opera, and song. This background would make them open to the similar world of culture that they would encounter in Cleveland.

Despite my mother's respect for my father's unappreciated intelligence, she persisted in a worldview based upon her version of history, a patchwork confection of émigré intellectuals and black intellectual outsiders that gave special meaning to her employment at Cleveland's Park Synagogue in University Circle. Needing work after my birth, my mother had applied for a position as a janitor at Park, an upwardly mobile synagogue designed by the already-distinguished architect Erich Mendelsohn and set back in the densely forested areas of Cleveland Heights' Severance neighborhood. Upon noticing her diploma and excellent academic record, three left-wing Jewish teachers insisted that she be hired as a teacher.

At Park, she encountered the economically, politically, and culturally expanding world of second- and third-generation immigrant Jews now wealthy from companies such as Leonard Ratner's Forest City. This encounter only reinforced her utopian view of Cleveland's—indeed, America's—possibilities for blacks. Park was a world that my father and the rest of our family knew only by reputation. Mother, however, found herself immersed in the synagogue, its teachers, and its members. These included the pianist Eunis Podis, members of Cleveland's wealthy Ratner family, and Rabbi Hillel Silver and his wife, Adele. Much of her admiration of elegant simplicity and her hatred of black middle-class flamboyance was reinforced by this contact with what seemed an exotic foreign culture. My mother cared little for fashion, but she often observed that these people dressed with a refinement the elegance of which lay in its simplicity. This was, of course, the result of the odd collision between a newly wealthy American class and Old World European distinctions of class, culture, and education. Here in Cleveland Heights, this émigré intellectual tradition was no longer marginal but triumphant—an example for other ethnically marginalized people. Part of her contempt for the inner city stemmed from the fact that its inhabitants had given up or never aspired to the level of achievement she saw at Park.

I remember only bits and pieces of the educational artifacts with which my mother showered me five years after she started working at Park, when I began elementary school. However, my memories of songs about dreidels, the symbolic meanings of the dishes served at the Passover meal, the establishment of a family life on the kibbutzim, and the celebration of Yom Kippur, Rosh Hashanah, and Hanukkah all coalesce in a vision of a particular culture for me. The children's books she brought home concerning the settlement of Israel after the war and the emergence of a generation of native Israelis called sabras (after a fruit that is sweet and soft on the inside but prickly on the outside) gave me, as an eight- or nine-year-old school boy, a physical and historical reality of a faraway land. Similarly, the Jewish holidays evoked the seasons of the year—the beginnings of spring, fall-time harvest, and the regeneration of the year—far more vividly than did the rituals of Easter and Christmas, which I celebrated during the year.

I naively grasped my mother's image of Judaism because it had a factual quality that gave it a powerful, if mysterious, appeal. And this mystery was reinforced by the synagogue's concealment behind a barrier of trees and shrubs. To be sure, my mother was not witness to the daily lives of Jews, which could by no means be stereotyped or generalized. What she carried in her mind was a romantic image.

I would recall my first indirect encounter with this world when I graduated from University School. I entered Park Synagogue for the first and only time as a high school senior to hear Senator J. William Fulbright talk about American foreign policy in Vietnam in the summer of 1968 on the night that Lyndon Johnson announced his decision not to seek a second term in office. As I put on a black yarmulke, I realized that I was entering a culture that was foreign to me, which I had only encountered in a secondhand way. Behind me, someone mentioned half jokingly, half sarcastically, that, whatever his appeal to northeastern liberals, Fulbright had historically catered to his segregationist southern constituency to maintain his electoral base. This was the Jewish intellect I encountered at prep school and would find at Yale and Chicago: ironic, witty, and skeptical of all mystifications—such as my mother's.

Even in elementary school, I gradually saw that the culture-filled world of my youth was one that my mother had herself been pondering and confecting for some time. The "good situations" in which my parents placed me inevitably confronted me with just what it was that she was after. There, in the hallways of the two-story Cleveland Institute of Music, where conservatory students could be heard playing classical music, I saw the children of white and Jewish professionals—many of them politically liberal—who had moved far beyond even the still partially Jewish suburban communities of Ludlow and Milverton deep into Shaker Heights and Cleveland Heights. I would see them again at Western Reserve in summer school. These voluble, articulate, fresh-faced children already had a command of reading and a vocabulary that transcended the classroom's demands. What my mother wished for for her family, and for her children in particular, was the confidence and dignity of learned people who had acquired a certain intellectual mastery. To be sure, this mastery must have existed somewhere in the black world of the doctors and lawyers in Cleveland. But working-class people like my parents seemed to have no access to—indeed, no knowledge of—such circles.

My mother interpreted the self-confidence of the doctors she saw walking around University Circle as a sign of their participation in a larger world of culture. She found this confidence in every aspect of their lives: oddly, even in the waywardness with which the professors let their grass grow tall in the academic neighborhoods of Cleveland Heights along Lee. These professors were too high minded, too busy writing books, to regularly tend to their lawns.

I was wholly taken in by my mother's vision of the reality of black Cleveland—an urban world that seemed alternately to strangle and expel our family. I carried the cultural world of our Saturday morning breakfasts in my head like one of the ornate Persian tapestries that I had seen on the walls of the Cleveland Art Museum during our Sunday afternoon visits to University Circle. This world and its points of reference—Germany, Columbia, Morningside Heights, and Greensboro—made me already at nine and ten years old a citizen of somewhere besides Mount Pleasant. It did not matter that I was instructed to follow a direct path to Robert Fulton Elementary School; I could have pursued no other. I was thoroughly distracted from the street by the world within my head. I can remember tripping and falling because my attention was directed not ahead but within. My knees were frequently bloody and scabbed, but I did not have to be told that such missteps were less dangerous than those leading to the black urban world: the world of tiny apartments not owned by their inhabitants where one did not study music, and where it was becoming unsafe to linger outside at night. We would be among black people whose fathers did not work or who did not have fathers—among the single men with liquor on their breath who drifted in and out of Abbot's barbershop on Saturday afternoons when my father and I had our hair cut. These people lived apart from the real world of culture that gave our Saturday breakfast table its glow.

In the mid-fifties Robert Fulton Elementary School still showed signs of Mount Pleasant's earlier rural character. My mother mildly approved of the school's largely white faculty, who were known for their competence in teaching basic skills. These teachers mechanically taught me reading, writing, and arithmetic in a series of routines: recitation, blackboard assignments, worksheets, and speed tests. They watched carefully for slips of accuracy and pace. We were drilled endlessly on our multiplication tables, and in the evenings I was drilled even more intensely at home. My mother created what seemed to be bottom-less stacks of flash cards made from the dividers of egg cartons. Between the hours of six and seven in the evening, I was confronted with these cards in every conceivable order. My mistakes were the basis for further drilling under the pretence of conversation with my mother at breakfast the next morning. I found these exercises disheartening. I could not imagine that these flash cards had anything to do with the culture my mother exalted.

And in some sense my mother confirmed my intuition. Although my mother found the school adequate, it was not, to her mind, first rate. Robert Fulton Elementary School, I was glad to find out from her, was not exactly the real world. In the evening when she watched me bathe and spoke admiringly of John Dewey and the Laboratory School at the University of Chicago, I got the message straight from the shoulder, with New England directness. I must learn the basics but know that education consisted of something more. For four years, I did well in all my subjects except writing and art. And here my mother took up my cause. Every summer for long hours, she worked with me—fruit-lessly—on my writing. Yet she had little use for my teachers' complaints about my artwork. After four years of self-restraint, she unleashed herself upon a newly hired fourth-grade teacher who was horrified to find herself accused of infringing upon what my mother pointedly described as my "vision of the world."

CHAPTER THREE

My Father's House

Unlike my mother, my father insisted that high-minded concerns did not excuse even a professor from failing to cut the grass, trim the lawn's edges, hose the cuttings down the driveway, and sweep them down the sidewalk every Saturday afternoon in the summer. My parents rarely argued their differing views of the world before us children. These noisy (periodically hushed) debates took place early in the morning, when my older sister and I were presumed to be asleep. My mother's emphasis on the German high culture that she was seeing at Park, and my father's view of the world from the school boiler rooms cast different nuances on their shared assumptions. For my father, Cleveland's political reality was the conflicts between the black janitors and Polish custodians jockeying for better-paying positions with the board of education, and between the Slovak- and German-dominated unions that kept Negroes out of the trades and thus the city's lucrative and expanding construction industry. Cleveland's reality was its black East Side and white West Side, and wealthy eastern suburbs that kept out blacks, eastern European immigrants, Jews, and Catholics through explicit or tacit means. Cleveland's reality was the numbers runners who managed huge amounts of money in the ghetto's underground economy and the organized crime groups associated with the building trades. My father saw the new class of Jewish European contractors and entrepreneurs such as the Ratners as one more bloc—neither more nor less sympathetic to blacks—in the city's traditional New England–based (in reality, Yale-educated) elite. The Jewish newcomers to the city were beginning to gain access to Cleveland's most exclusive country clubs. He knew from friends, probably black housekeepers and waiters at country clubs, that the new elite's children were increasingly attending the city's schools for the wealthy, such as University School. The richest, like a much earlier generation of wealthy WASPS, were gathering in Shaker Heights and Cleveland Heights, as well as in the farther-flung fields of Beachwood and Pepper Pike. Polite as he might be to my mother's co-workers at Park, he retained a grim sense of his social distance from such people. He recognized that in their world he was a black boy recently up from the South scraping out a lower-middle-class life, making quite a good living (for a black worker) from an unexpectedly generous postwar economic boom.

Although he would never say it out loud, my mother's world of culture—compelling as it was in the singing of Roland Hayes, Paul Robeson, and Marian Anderson—belonged mainly to the intellectual, artistic, and literary aspirations of the tiny intelligentsia based in the most progressive and wealthiest congregations such as Park Synagogue, cultivated German Jewish families such as the Ratners, and newcomer businessmen such as Milton Wolf. This sensitivity to these distinctions also characterized his perception of the clique of left-wing women who had hired my mother at Park. My father's conception of culture was tempered by his fear of radical politics, his feeling that the Communist Party had betrayed Robeson and Du Bois, and later by his own observations of left-wing organizers in the plants and the experience of Cleveland radicals during the McCarthy era. Although he acknowledged the increasing new opportunities for blacks in the North, he maintained his suspicions of whites on the Left as well as the Right, the McCarthys and the Bilbos. Clarence Richards was in his own way hopeful but not deluded. This political vision accounted for the wariness with which he tempered my mother's increasing but vague left-wing radicalism and enjoined me against cynicism. The world had become, he might say, a better place for blacks; however, their lives still might be ruined by politics. He watched my later participation in the peace and civil rights movement with wariness. Sign nothing, he warned. Avoid the pamphlet literature.

When I became a professor at Colgate, I was welcomed by Joseph Slater, an eminent scholar of Emerson's letters and the son of a wealthy Shaker Heights family. Their home had not been far from University Schoool's Claythorne and Brantley campus. When I met him, he was entering his senior years and only a year or so away from retirement. Slater had in the thirties and forties been a card-carrying communist who experimented with what my mother called city life. He went downtown to the jazz and blues joints as blithely as he involved himself in the Communist Party and the unions, and he eagerly questioned me about my parents' participation in Cleveland's jazz and blues scene. I was only partially horrified. My mother talked about these places out of the side of her mouth as she described my aunt and her successful hairdresser friend going to the downtown clubs and sitting on the laps of white men. Proper middle-class black people—especially those who aspired to a bourgeois life-style, like my father—knew the dangers of these activities. For this reason, he cautioned my mother against the political radicalism and cultural enthusiasms of the people who had hired her. They were not for bourgeois black people who raised children and paid mortgages.

My father's wariness arose from the black mother wit of Cleveland in the fifties, and my father turned the folk skepticism of the ghetto against my mother's high-mindedness. He would respond to her enthusiastic tirades at the dinner table with the language of Glenville and Central streets, referring perhaps to the appearance of a new "deuce and a quarter" (the ghetto name for an Electra 225) in a nearby driveway. In response to her angry retorts, he would end on an only partly humorous note: "These are colored people, baby. This is the way that colored people live."

To be sure, my father supported our middle-class lifestyle. He did not smoke, drink, gamble, consort with women, or fail to attend church regularly. His most visible moral weakness was the weekly half gallon of peach ice cream that we shared on Friday spring evenings after dinner. He promoted his children's education, scrutinized any work I did, criticized my bad habits, taught me the most basic household skills, laughed at my foolishness, and scolded me for my laziness. He could in the face of a disobedient child be a stern man. However, he was also wise about human life in a way that my mother understood but could not admit before us children.

He knew enough about human nature to allow himself some vanities. This wisdom allowed him to continue as a dandy. On Saturday afternoons, he polished his shoes to a deep resonant shine. Later, he meticulously shaved and trimmed his moustache with a single-edged razor, which he periodically stropped. On Sundays after breakfast, he carefully dressed himself in his gray or navy suit, which he wore with a striped or dotted silk tie against a stiffly starched white shirt that my mother had ironed the previous Saturday afternoon.

From his point of view, my mother was not only a creature of culture; she was also his conquest. I suspect that she had an erotic fantasy life that rivaled her intellectual ambitions, and that she liked him watching her as she talked and fluttered through the house. She was the princess he had captured and taken away for himself. Through his eyes, she saw herself with an aesthetic and intellectual interest that was more than mere vanity: it was an assertion of her worth in a white world that ruthlessly denied her personhood on the streets, in the schools, and in the stores downtown.

I could not be kept in the house forever, and my trips to the homes of my friends provided a new perspective on my mother's view of the coming collapse of Negro life in Mount Pleasant. I had a set of friends—Steven Wright, Carl Wallace, and Martha Jewett—largely chosen by my mother; however, when I went to their homes, I saw things that my mother would not have discussed with me at our dinner table or in our conversations at night before bed. No one else seemed to fear the end of the world; my friends and their families blithely ignored the coming urban apocalypse that my mother foresaw for the black people of the community. Around the corner and down the block in Mount Pleasant, things seemed, at least to me, to be just fine. Walking into my friends' duplex and tenement apartments, I entered the world into which my family feared we would fall. In the closets were leather coats for Saturday nights, and silk dresses for Sunday. Their parents smoked, and on Monday afternoons, one might see a small gin bottle left on the kitchen table from the weekend, miraculously unscathed. Their children wore blue jeans to school, contrary to my mother's dicta for our family. These children belonged to a world of luxury unlike my plain existence at home. They ate the chitterlings and hog maws their mothers cooked on New Year's Day and accompanied their families to baseball and football games at the Cleveland stadium, where their fathers might enjoy a flask of whisky hidden in the pocket of a long cashmere or leather coat. For Christmas they received so much that they shared their bounty with me, and I looked forward to their surplus booty: up-to-date baseballs cards (from the doubles and triples in their collections) and comic books (in particular, *The Flash, Green Lantern, The Justice League of America,* and *Wonder Woman*).

My classes were, in the mid-fifties, racially integrated by the remaining eastern European and German children who had not moved to Cleveland's West Side or southwest suburbs. The Jews, on the other hand, had moved to Shaker Heights and Cleveland Heights. My perception of white people was that they were all moving to the eastern suburbs from Cleveland. The darkening of the school's population apparently bothered my mother too. Deeply concerned about the education of her oldest child, my mother met with my principal, Mrs. Lord, at least every two weeks to check on my progress.

Everything about my daily experience with my best friends seemed to shout that my family and its values could not be taken seriously. These values had, I noticed, not made me more generous or polite than my friends. Spending recess on the playground, walking home for lunch, or playing games during gym, I was as noisy, conniving, and wayward as anyone else. In fact, my parents' values seemed to make me an outsider. Despite their parents' inattention, my friends seemed to thrive in ways that I did not. By the time we reached the second or third grade, I envied my peers their athletic grace—the casual ease with which they shot marbles, swept up a handful of jacks, or ascended in the air toward the basketball hoop as if drawn from the shoulders, their feet casually dangling. In races, their slender bodies—even those of the girls in dresses—shot by me with ease. They could hit a baseball to the opposite side of the outfield or throw a football in—it seemed to me—the manner of the pros, high in the air, spinning as if traveling along a cord, finally dropping to a designated spot thirty or forty yards away.

I competed academically to achieve credibility in the classroom that I would never win out on the street. With more energy than finesse, I worked my way up to the most advanced groups in arithmetic and reading, always a little piqued that my friends seemed to excel so effortlessly. My urge to succeed led me to become as obsessed as my mother over Major Work. A daydreaming reader forbidden to enter the streets, I strove to become gifted. I did not score high enough on the IQ test to be admitted in the second grade and succeeded, to my classmates' bewilderment, only in the fourth grade. A number of my Robert Fulton classmates would enter this program in seventh grade, but none of my friends were contending for entrance early in elementary school. From second to third grade, my concern was a joke among my friends, who teased me, nicknaming me "Major Work." If a person could be such an entity, then I was.

My initial failure to enter the program frustrated me. Thoroughly confused, I finally turned to my all-purpose source of information, the *Child Craft* encyclopedia, the final volumes of which included information on child-rearing. I did not understand many of the books that I tried to read as a child, but focused on the pressing question of my intelligence, I grasped enough of what the *Child Craft* volume had to say about "gifted" children to be scared out of my wits. For once, I read an adult text with enough care and critical reflection to understand it, and I received the shock of my life. I had believed the weak, slender bespectacled figure such as myself to be the prototypical gifted child. Yet the clumsy, daydreaming person I had become was, the encyclopedia insisted, not the prototype of the gifted young person. To the contrary, the gifted child was often physically well developed, adept in his or her social relations with others, and emotionally stable—often more so than his or her fellows. Indeed, intellectual gifts were simply one more sign of advanced childhood development. Carl, Martha, and Steven were far more likely candidates for giftedness than I. Such well-adjusted people did not have to pursue an advanced academic program; it would pursue them. Whatever I was, I fit into no standard mold for superiority.

I came to understand that I was not a gifted person but a smart-aleck pre-tender, an academic hustler of sorts. Gifted people dominate the world around them, and my friends were mastering the worlds of sports, play, school friend-ships, and even extracurricular activities such as plays, in which I did not participate. It was impossible for me to imagine myself being elected a class president, vice president, or secretary like Carl or Martha. Yet according to the *Child Craft* articles on gifted children, this was the kind of mastery that the truly intelligent young person possessed. This made me angry. For the first time it occurred to me that I, not the rest of the world around me, was marginal.

I gathered that on our block on 137th Street in Mount Pleasant, my parents were considered odd. The postman walking down the street on Saturday morning winked at me. I suspect that their perception of their oddness led to conflicts that I did not understand. At the corner of 137th and Abel was a modernist house designed, built, and owned by a black architect. No one—not even my parents—could deny that they represented the highest level of black achievement. His daughter Aleta—a dark, attractive girl—was in my class at Fulton. Her parents, successful, urbane people, had obvious contempt for mine. She was arrogant and intolerant, as full of her parents' self-importance as I was of my mother's claims to cultural superiority, and I disliked her immensely. By the third grade, we seemed always to be fighting over something that I could never define. She was snubbing me, although I was too inept and distracted to know how she was doing it. For some reason, the erect, self-assured way she walked made me mad.

At some point in the second or third grade, I made friends with Mike, the son of a ne'er-do-well black World War II veteran who could not support his swarm of children and meek Japanese wife. Mike did what he pleased. I often saw him urinating in the empty field at the northern end of our block as I walked home from school or sticking a detached extended television antenna into tomatoes and pears or stealing a Snickers candy bar or a large bag of M&M's at the Fisher's Supermarket on 140th and Kinsman.

His father, Mike once told me, was in "policy." Seeing my uncomprehending look, he stared at me closely and instructed me to tell no one what he had said. "What," I asked my mother as soon as I got home, was "policy?" Did Mike mean that his father sold insurance? My mother's answer stopped me cold. Mike's father was a runner: he handled the bets of people who gambled daily in the illegal numbers game. Mob bosses ran these games, ruthlessly enforcing bad debts with shootings and beatings. My parents often discussed this activity when the *Cleveland Press* reported the arrests of these hoodlums. Thugs policed the actual games themselves. They, in turn, were defended by the sharpie black lawyers who conducted their practices in the city. Who, she asked, did I think I was? Mike knew the streets and had sized me up. Did I think that I could live by my wits out in Mount Pleasant? Unable to fight, ignorant of the realities of Kinsman and 140th, I was a mark. Mike would eventually take, she continued, whatever he wanted from me—I couldn't imagine anything I had that he would want—and beat me up. I was immediately afraid not only of him—I expected him to be coming after me soon enough—but of anyone else like him.

Now frightened, I began to heed the newcomers from the inner city at Robert Fulton. I was, I gradually realized, a moving target. The tough kids around me were not slow to notice this. During my last year at Robert Fulton, a small boy dressed in ragged woolen shirts and jeans began to follow me, punching and tripping me whenever we were alone. He waited for me at the close of school and every afternoon gave me a worse beating. He was perfectly silent, but from his intense constant observation of my movements, I surmised he was angry. I had abused him, had violated some code. Just how, I did not know. Perhaps he did not like the way I walked. Fighting was forbidden in my family, but this seemed to me a special case. I told my mother about the problem, and she determined that my father should pick me up the next day. She interpreted this situation in an abstractly formal way, the legalism of which shocked me. My fighting was dangerous. I might be hurt, but in the unlikely event that I hurt my attacker (even in self-defense), our family's property, she argued, might be at stake. My parents, she informed me, were property owners and therefore vulnerable to a costly insurance claim by my attacker's parents or an even costlier legal suit. I found her logic chilling. I had not thought that our house was at stake on the playground, and that my parents could not protect me there.

The next day my father picked me up. It was a good thing, for I just made it to the car before my attacker could overtake me. Shocked, my would-be assailant turned on his heel, escaping down Abel. I was amazed at how fast he covered ground, and he was well beyond 135th Street before my father and I caught up to him in the car. From there he dipped and bobbed westward through Mount Pleasant's back streets and alleys toward Woodland Hills. A few times we came upon other boys who looked much like him, and it occurred to me that Mike would necessarily know the streets well. I had never looked hard at Mike's face, and for some reason, I began to think that my attacker might be Mike. As I looked out the window at the boys going home, I grew increasingly excited. Indeed, Mike seemed to be everywhere. As we chased my attacker, I realized how many boys his age there were in Mount Pleasant. He was a creature of the streets in a way that I would never be, even if I were to live there my entire life. He had obviously hidden before like this—perhaps from shopkeepers or the police. His disappearance, preceded by the initial flurry of escape, was as deft and mysterious as the magician's tricks I had seen at the 140th and Kinsman branch of the Cleveland Public Library party for children who had read and reported on ten books the previous summer. (In response to my query, the performer averred that magicians never tell the secrets of their tricks.) By the time we got to Woodland Hills Park, I conceded that my assailant had vanished, leaving only my fear. Silent and tight lipped, my father drove me back home. He had lost some hours of overtime and was not pleased. I was dumbfounded. I was as afraid of the city, its Negroes, and its streets as my parents were. I understood why they kept me at home. I did not now particularly care to leave the house.

After this incident, my father paid special attention to me during our Saturday chores, keeping me by his side as we worked. On those mornings I watched as he puttered about the garage in search of tools with which to change the car's oil, set the spark plugs, or rotate the tires. After my music lessons he would watch me cut the lawn. Off to the side he might trim the bushes, weed the tree lawn's curb, or repair a loose step on the porch. He assigned me minor tasks to help him with. As I cut the grass, moving back and forth in long rows, he checked my work, looking carefully for spots I had missed. He quickly noticed how clumsy I was with tools, and how sloppily I pushed the lawn mower along overlapping rows of grass

Sometime in midsummer, I noticed him looking directly into my face as I worked. In the past, he had warned me about my ability to become so easily distracted, my inability to concentrate. At that moment, I thought that he was about to warn me again. Instead, he looked at me casually and inquired whether I knew that there was a world beyond the books in my room and the library on 140th and Kinsman. Before I could answer, he remarked that in 1915 he had been born in Cincinnati, Ohio, to a ditchdigger and—somewhat improbably, it seemed to me—his educated stay-at-home wife. My father had lived briefly in Cincinnati, and later in Winchester, Kentucky, during the twenties and thirties. At the height of the Depression in the thirties, his father, Lucian, could not always feed his wife and eight children. On payday—"when the eagle flew," as he might say—Lucian might bring home a steak. On the other weekdays, the children would make do with bread and jam or mayonnaise with a glass of water. For a little while in the mid-thirties, four or five of the brothers shared a large mattress with a cat. Romping on the bed one morning after awakening, the brothers discovered the cat's incomprehensibly stiff body. The cat was dead.

Everything that lives dies, my father observed. Did I know that I would die? Death was something with which his schoolmates had been acquainted. During the typhoid epidemic of 1923, in the wake of warnings about the town's water, the disease had struck Winchester, killing many of the black children his age. When their temperatures passed 102 degrees, he said, the children usually died. Their stiff bodies wrapped in white were lifted into ambulances and were never seen again. His mother, my grandmother Julia, told eight-year-old Clarence Richards that "we do not come here to stay." And his little friends were no more. Years later, his father Lucian died in bed, howling with pain, his stomach perforated with ulcers. Downstairs, his wife and children listened helplessly. This might have been predicted. Like me, my father observed dryly, Lucian was always gobbling his food.

My father's most lasting impression of Kentucky State was the ruthless domination of blacks over blacks. Some of this could be funny. Adopting a stiff, upright stance in the garage, he imitated a young black PhD fresh from Indiana University. (Negroes were barred from graduate study at the University of Kentucky, and the young professor postured, attempting to embody his provincial conception of a learned man.) Announcing his imitation of the young ass, my father held a forefinger upright like a candle, moving it horizontally from side to side as well as now and again behind his back. Some of this was not funny. After an academically questionable first year, my father was dismissed from the school. "You are a pauper, Richards," the dean had said. "Go home and work for the white people." When my father arrived home, Lucian was not there but at the barber shop, telling stories and playing cards.

What did I think life was really about? my father asked. Leaving Kentucky State in 1940, he returned home to Winchester then departed suddenly for

Hampton Institute in Virginia. "Something said, 'Go,'" he said. And he went. What did I think of that? he asked. I looked at him puzzled, my tongue tied. Satisfied by this response, he turned his back to me and drew up a length of the thick green garden hose. Placidly, he looked back at our brown-shingled house. At that moment it seemed a mansion.

CHAPTER FOUR

Coming of Age at
Alexander Hamilton Jr. High School

The shock of my father's remarks stayed with me for some time. My father typically silently tolerated my intellectual flights during our weekend conversations. Both of my parents were proud of my reading, as freewheeling and undisciplined as it was. My wildest flights of fancy were only rarely countered by common sense. My mother had defended my refusal to color within the lines in my first- and second-grade coloring books. She did this in the name of my vision of the world. My mother's permissiveness seemed natural given the way in which her own admiration of the German Jewish intellectual culture of the Ratners and Adele Silver flouted the day-to-day norms of the black people around her family. My own waywardness, I sensed, was implicitly guaranteed by the defiant way in which she talked about John Dewey and the founding of the University of Chicago Laboratory School as she bathed me. And this awareness allowed me a certain amount of space for fanciful play. I began, during the summer after the fifth grade, however, to realize that my parents—like the sharpies in their brightly colored suits out on Kinsman—possessed something of the quick intelligence of the streets themselves.

Strange as it may have seemed, they had succeeded as middle-class people by exercising even greater guile than their slick friends with leather coats and stolen luxury goods. Somehow my mother and father had outwitted the few pedantic teachers who had harassed them at Hampton and Kentucky State, the foremen who had endangered my father's life in the wartime dockyards of Newport News, and the handful of resentful supervising teachers at Park Synagogue. All this was accomplished with something like the wit with which Mike's father collected bad debts from innocents who had put their rent money on the wrong number the previous day. The utter necessity of this guile was ignored at one's own risk. Black life often presented black people with problems and paradoxes that defied rational explanation. The arbitrary power wielded by blacks against white people could be turned upon blacks. Did he think that white racism was particularly bad in Cleveland? my father once remarked in response to my mother's comments about a lurid article in the *Cleveland Press*. Some of his worst experiences, he went on to say, had been with black people. There was something worse than being a hoodlum in what my mother called "the city." One could be a fool.

My father's understanding of the various levels of the black world came from a more complicated family background than one would have suspected from his angry remarks about his wayward father and my mother's derision of the Richardses as a whole. Lucian's father was a descendant of Richardses, who were apparently descended from a slave and her white master. The Richardses were widely respected in the small town of Winchester, Kentucky, and they owned property. Lucian's siblings owned property and held office jobs, and my father's brothers attended college and theological school, becoming ministers, lawyers, and other white-collar workers. Lucian married Julia Gray, who came from another middle-class property-owning black family. Julia and her sister attended Berea College, which had been run by abolitionists before the Civil War. Julia's marriage to Lucian endowed the family with a large share of the land in the colored area of the town.

Much of what my father had to say suggested that he was smarter than he looked. Although he would never say this out loud, he knew that he and his immediate family were part of a black American history that had little to do with the Ratners and Park Synagogue. Indeed, such relations were only the tip of the iceberg of the black-Jewish patronage relationships. Of course such interracial relationships had existed in theater, radical politics, and the unions for some time. These were dangerous paths by which Du Bois and Robeson had entered a political hell.

He was also skeptical of my mother's grandiose claims about her family, the truth of which could not be ascertained. However, he did give credence to the central proposition of her story. The Williamses made much of the family patriarch, Jimmie Williams, a successful farmer in Weldon, North Carolina, who was the son of a distinguished white North Carolina lawyer. After a dispute with his father, Jimmie had gone to New York City, worked there in hotels as a busboy, and returned to North Carolina with sufficient money to buy a farm. By all accounts, his facial features and skin color were those of a white man.

The Williams family, according to family lore, had long enjoyed—apparently through Reconstruction and the post-Reconstruction era—privileges bestowed upon mulattos linked by kin to influential whites.

My father was himself the descendant of such a family and understood the social and political power that this light-skinned mulatto bourgeois identity retained in the mid-twentieth century. A brown-skinned man, he had clearly not been repelled by the "color-struck" women of the Williams clan, who taunted their cousin's brilliant black-skinned fiancé (a medical student who would become head of the surgery unit in his Dayton, Ohio, hospital during the sixties), calling him "*Crow*-Martie." Clarence Richards understood the residual prestige of the mulatto elite, even in the mid-twentieth century, when the black-skinned proletariat migrants to the North began to attain political power. He had, in his union with a smart, educated light-skinned woman from a prestigious mulatto family, established a shrewd conjugal alliance that would stand him in good stead throughout the second half of the twentieth century in black Cleveland.

The contradictions embraced by the mother wit of the race at the same time suggested that the black culture of the streets, the world of the city, could not be so easily dismissed. Both of my parents seemed to have absorbed enough of the black folk spirit of the poems of Robeson and the spirituals of Hayes to know that the world of what my mother dismissed as the city was an inescapable reality. And he knew that this conundrum was best embodied by anecdotes rather than political formulations.

My father as well as my mother could appeal to the wisdom of the folk. Working in the plants on Cleveland's southeast side, he had been partnered with an eastern European workmate immediately after him on the assembly line. The two had first warily felt each other out, only to gradually become friends. The assembly line could be a dangerous place during speed-ups and extended work stints. The two often saved each other from injury by rousing one another from drowsiness and alerting each other to sudden changes in procedures and the often volatile personal conflicts between blacks and whites in the factory.

His white friend eventually acquired a job as a manager in a new startup company in the city. My father went to the plant to apply for a job; he said this with a rising voice intended to dramatize his mood of expectancy. At this point, my mother turned her head and smirked. Coming into his friend's office, he shook hands with his erstwhile partner from the plant. Looking him straight in the eye with a smile, the white man announced to my father that "All my boys start off with a broom." My parents' discussions of the horrors of the plants always seemed to end in arguments; however, this story settled whatever disagreement between them seemed to be in the offing. The long ensuing silence suggested his purchase on a fundamental racial reality that my idealistic mother had to honor.

After nearly being beaten up in the Robert Fulton schoolyard, I mentally dredged up the warnings my father had given me. I would in the fourth grade walk directly into Cleveland's eastern European world as I entered Major Work classes at Boulevard Elementary, having finally passed the evaluation. I began to ponder the significance of this fact. My father had warned me about the inhospitable Czechs, Hungarians, and Poles who dominated life in Cleveland. In Murray Hill and Collinwood, their gangs forbade blacks to enter their neighborhoods, and black intruders had been badly beaten in the racial border areas. As in many northern cities in the fifties and early sixties, the immigrant Polish, Hungarian, and Serbian politicians dominated the city council, the board of education, and public services, dispensing political patronage to the blacks who did their bidding. As he drove on Saturdays and Sundays to perform weekend checks at the various East Side schools where he worked as a custodian (significantly, he was never assigned a school in Cleveland's all-white West Side), my father pointed out to me such neighborhoods, with their large gray churches, aromatic bakeries, and meticulously kept front lawns. As I thought about Boulevard on Kinsman and East 93rd Street, it became clear to me that my acceptance to Major Work meant that I would be entering this volatile eastern European immigrant world—a sphere different from the Cleveland Institute of Music and the settlement house, where I spent two hours weekly with the friendly, voluble children of Jewish professors, lawyers, and doctors.

Cleveland's academic program for gifted children had been founded in the twenties to provide an accelerated curriculum for students whose abilities exceeded standard classroom teaching. Anticipating Boulevard, I reflected on the ethnic loyalties of my parents. Eccentric as they were, they belonged to the world of black Mount Pleasant. They had friends there; on summer evenings, they walked down 137th Street, bordered by its sycamores, maples, and elms whose autumn leaves would fall to be swept, gathered, and burned in ash-blackened backyard oil cans. They chatted with Mr. Hirsch, a large black man who worked, I think, as a waiter at a downtown men's club, pausing as he leisurely smoked a cigar in front of his large front lawn on 137th Street. Whatever my parents thought of the world of Mount Pleasant, it was incontestably theirs. This was particularly true in the early sixties as some of the community's prominent members became known not only throughout the city and state but sometimes beyond.

As I contemplated the fullness of Cleveland's Polish, Hungarian, and Serbian world, I realized the meaning of rejecting a racial identity: of declaring my marginality to a blackness that was so fully and complexly defined in city life. There was no exit from the house of race. Individuality, I began to see, was not only my mother's hymn to the far-off world of Park Synagogue, Max Ratner's expansive clan, and earnest black graduate students at the University of Chicago; it was also my father's grimace as he watched me carry a saw, or a nameless black boy beating me to the limit of my senses in the playground of Robert Fulton Elementary School. For the entire summer after fifth grade, I had felt that the world of Cleveland was trying to communicate something to me. But now, contemplating a future on 93rd Street amid the white Slavs of the Boulevard district, I got the point. I was black. And everyone knew what it was to be black in Cleveland.

In the fall of 1960, I began school at Boulevard Elementary. I left Mount Pleasant on the No. 14 bus and rode down Kinsman to 93rd Street, where from the bottom of a green hill I saw my new school. It was a sprawling red-brick structure across the street from the hill I had just descended. Riding the bus from Mount Pleasant, I had left the black neighborhood that extended to Woodland Hills and passed through a gray cityscape of small stores, parks, and decaying bungalows. Looking to the left or right or over my shoulder, I saw my fellow passengers—older white men and women—reading newspapers in Polish, German, and Czech and I found myself in a new world. I observed old women shopping, pulling their wire carts to market, an image similar to those I might have seen in the *World Book Encyclopedia*'s entries for Krakow and Warsaw. They bustled past me, heads down, muttering to themselves, angrily oblivious to my presence. Walking to the school, I might see a diminutive elderly woman—Polish, Hungarian, or Serbian—approach a nun and kiss the ring on her finger. The tiny old woman would stoop as the nun, her black robes billowing in the wind, extended her hand.

I had seen glimmers of this life during drives with my father. Now these foreign sights defined me as a stranger. Looking around me, I took in these alien gestures and objects with fresh incomprehension. My white female classmates at Boulevard wore golden crucifixes suspended on thin chains around their necks. In moments of nervousness or boredom, they reached into a pocket to extract prayer beads of coral, green, and earthy brown. In previous years, I had largely been aware of the city's white Anglo, Irish, and European presence from the names of politicians: Celebreze, Locher, McAllister. In my new classroom, I encountered people with equally bizarre names. I had never sensed that actual people lived intimately with the foreign sounds and symbols that surrounded me.

During my first week at school, I observed my physical setting as often as I watched my fellows. Students were seated four a piece at neatly arranged tables. Many of them worked together on class projects. When formal recitations ended, they gathered in small groups, talking and writing.

Our reading classes demanded that we read books by ourselves and discuss them in small groups. We kept notebooks in which we listed the parts of speech that we encountered: nouns, verbs, adjectives. We also listed the basic figures of speech: similes, symbols, and metaphors. One of our teachers, a bespectacled woman named Mrs. Haberland, had literally escaped her family, household, and neighborhood in eastern Ohio's Amish community to marry a young engineer and forge a new existence for herself. She had left the black homemade clothing, horse-drawn buggies, and straw hats of her kinsmen to, as she put it, join the modern world. Every morning she chalked a new aphorism or proverb on the blackboard: "Who will watch the police?" written in Latin or "The wheels of the gods grind slowly but they grind exceedingly small." Some of these were provocations, such as the admonition of the Spartan mothers to their soldier sons: "Come back with your shield or on it." She never discussed these sayings with the class but simply wrote them on the blackboard to be read. I never entered the class in the morning without sitting down, looking at the new saying, and pondering it deeply. She was the first intellectual I ever knew: it was of the greatest importance to me that early in life she had declared herself an exceptional person unique among the citizens of her inbred traditional world.

The Major Work classroom had special meaning for me. This room seemed familiar to me from the large reading halls in the downtown library and the enclosures for the display and contemplation of paintings and sculptures in the Cleveland Museum of Art, as well as the practice rooms at the Cleveland settlement house. These spaces separated people in ways that introduced them not to each other but to their individual abilities to make sense of the world. From the beginning, my classmates seemed a distraction to me. It was the shelves and shelves of books along the wall that immediately drew my attention. And right away, I began to spend all my free time between classes reading whatever attracted my notice as I drifted along the shelves.

I could not, however, ignore those classmates who impressed me in spite of my attempts to dismiss them. Many were one or two years ahead of me.

There was Dennis Valenzino, an Italian two years older than I. I noticed him at once: a congenial but businesslike fellow respected by the other students, one of the class officers, but friendly to all. In the fifth and sixth grades, he carried a brown briefcase. On special occasions, Donald Bowers, a little taller and thicker than I, performed experiments with arc lamps in the darkened classroom. Bobby Pawlek, a lanky tow-headed boy, could beat anyone in the class at chess. Finally there was a gentle girl named Dale Weimer who wore her brown-blonde hair cut like the rim of a bowl across her forehead. She wore short dresses, black leotards, and velvet shoes shaped like ballet slippers. She held the attention of the teacher during discussions about her group's reading. I gazed at these young people involuntarily. By the end of the first week, it had become brutally clear that I would not attract any particular interest from my classmates or teacher. No one but me was particularly excited by the thoughts running through my head as I read the books I pulled from the wall. And it now occurred to me that there was no reason why they should be.

I saw no hope of triumphing over this swarm of competitors—an unsettling insight. I had fancied myself a special person, a gifted individual, if not a consistently excellent student; however, here in the midst of other gifted young people, I was not particularly exceptional. As I thought the matter over, I realized that my sense of exceptionality had always been located less in the world around me than in remembered and imagined images drawn from books. Late at night or on drowsy afternoons, I had located myself in a world of these absorbed animals, things, places, and people: species of fish, varieties of monkeys, frontier families, geometry, Robert Fulton and the steam engine, the Mayan calendar, the building of Brasília, Peter the First, the travels of Marco Polo, the charts of the geological ages, and horse raising on Chincoteague Island.

I grasped all this in three weeks, and by the time of our first special-interest talk, I was filled with fear, anger, resentment, and despair. Special-interest talks were twenty-minute oral presentations on a topic that the student had extensively researched. All the students in the class graded these talks. A supremely excellent talk could receive an A-plus only by a unanimous vote. Dale Weimer's talk on a subject I have long since forgotten met with acclaim from our classmates. She was immediately given an A. A second vote was held to determine whether she should receive an A-plus. Filled with spite, I was the only one who voted against the grade. The class and teacher were shocked. William West, a very smart, popular black student, talked my vote over with me during recess. At first I suspected that the teacher might have sent him to me. After I got to know him, however, I realized that he was thoughtful enough to have come on his own. At any rate, I refused to change my judgment. Dale Weimer had to settle for an A. I took a bitter satisfaction in this. For a moment, my position in the class seemed a little more promising.

The class as a whole, however, was outraged, angered—it seemed to me—more by the flouting of their collective will than by any real concern for Dale Weimer. And their anger deepened when I refused to change the grade and bitterly defended my judgment to anyone who dared question it. Their contempt took the form of ostracism. After the talk, I was generally left alone. No one invited me to participate in class projects, and I spent my time reading the classroom's encyclopedias and geography atlases.

I became a member of the class hierarchy's lowest tier. Although I was interested in books, my scattered and undisciplined reading had no official sanction. Indeed, the history and fiction reading I did in between classes seemed like one more stroke of defiance in the face of my academic betters. As I grew more estranged from my classmates, I realized the ways in which they were as odd to me as I was to them, and I began to explore this oddity in my imagination. They reminded me of the green winding plants in the only other place where I had seen so many eastern European people for any length of time: Segelin's, a large garden-supply store near our church, Antioch Baptist, on 89th and Cedar. My father and I often went there on Sunday afternoons after church, often coming upon an orange or pink flower, a brilliant splash of color amid the planted pots, peat moss, and plastic sacks of fertilizer around it. In Segelin's my father had once pointed out to me the bulbous pink head of Louis Seltzer, the editor of the sensationalist *Cleveland Press*. Looking at him, I remembered Janet Lave, who was a year or so behind me in my class at Boulevard. She was very blonde; her arms, pink with a slight glow, were covered with fine brown hair. She probably was as afraid of me as of any other black from the city. Looking at her, I thought of her glow as tropical, brightly poisonous. She was like some hothouse flower, almost luminescent.

I now took advantage of my already acknowledged oddness to do whatever odd things I pleased. And with this bizarre sanction, I approached Janice one day to inquire what she had done over the weekend. She informed me that she and her family had gone to Sokol Tyrs, a neighborhood community center where she practiced gymnastics. I tried to imagine her in a black leotard on a trampoline. I must have stared at her as I did so, for she returned my look, blushing, as if the privacy of her neighborhood life, which was wholly off limits to blacks, had been invaded. Summoning up an image of Janice in her tights, I had clearly crossed a racial line.

There was only one radio in the house, and I did not listen to the R&B and jazz that were beginning to make their way onto the local airwaves. I was aware of the new black music from the quick dance steps that two black girls in short dresses might execute between classes or during recess. My father listened to little music during the week, but on Saturdays and Sundays in the car, I would listen with him to big band music or the Texaco Opera program. For me, music was primarily piano practice and the piano recitals that occurred once or twice a semester at Boulevard.

However, I liked practicing the piano as I waited for dinner. I enjoyed the recitals, and my parents came to them with some relief that I was competently performing some socially acceptable activity. They usually arrived at the auditorium individually. My mother would wear a simple flowered dress. The white principal, Mrs. Vitek, who stood greeting parents at the door, never acknowledged her. Mom would sit inconspicuously in the front row. My father, whose schedule kept him at work until late afternoon, would arrive after the event had begun. Under his long dark woolen coat, he wore a white shirt, black worsted pants, and a tie. To my eye, he walked with the easy dignity of the bank officers at Society National. Sitting at the back of the auditorium, he carried himself with a gracefulness that made him inconspicuous in a largely white audience. He too went unacknowledged by the principal.

I realized for the first time that for all my parents' love for Cleveland and all its possibilities, they were strangers at Boulevard. When my father became an assistant custodian at Robert Fulton in Mount Pleasant, my sister Patrice had gone to the principal, Mrs. Lord, and announced that Dad had taken control of the school. My father had laughed at my sister's assertion when he recounted it at dinner. Robert Fulton, however, was for the most part black. This joke, it was clear to me, would not have been funny to the white faculty and administration now sitting in the auditorium at Boulevard. Mrs. Lord was a congenial, generous person, and my mother had taken advantage of her own personal charm and cultivation to establish a personal relationship with the principal as a means of monitoring my progress. My mother shared no such understanding with Boulevard's principal, a German woman in her mid-forties securely enmeshed within her ethnic enclave. Indeed, my mother, as far as I know, never said more than a few words to her.

I entered the immigrant European world of Boulevard as an outsider with my usual cantankerousness, staking my claim to importance among my fellows.

This aggressiveness, I think, accounts, for whatever success I finally experienced in the program. It certainly explains the eagerness with which I seized upon French as a foreign language, a code that sorted people out not by color but by their powers of comprehension. I had earlier conceived of languages as a set of rules and sentence structures, but never as a vehicle of custom and tradition. French was the language of the songs we sang in class: "Alouette," "Sur le Pont d'Avignon," "Savez-Vous Planter les Chous?" These songs I later heard sung by Africans, French people, and Creoles. They were known by all young French-speaking students, whether in French Central Africa, Paris, or Martinique.

In the French classroom, we sat with our chairs arranged along the walls in a semi-circle. As we memorized the names of fruits, vegetables, meats, the rooms of a house, dining utensils, kitchenware, and tools, this universal world appeared to me first in imagery and later in sound and voice. As we repeated the words—*le pamplemousse, la pomme, la fourchette, le lavabos*—French became not only a vehicle of expression but a means of sight, a set of visual markers, a window looking out over worlds thousands of miles away. Standing in a fruit market in Libreville, Gabon, I asked for *une pastèque* and received a large round green fruit. I had known that there was such a word, but not that it really stood for such a thing. Through the magical reality of words, I came to believe at Boulevard that I would gain access to other worlds. By the agency of words, I would escape Cleveland.

About a year after I entered Boulevard, when I was in the sixth grade, my parents—alarmed at the deterioration of the Mount Pleasant neighbor-hood—moved our family farther southeast to the Lee-Harvard community, which had only recently been integrated. The movement of blacks into this area had first provoked violence among white residents. Crosses were burned on lawns, and harsh words spoken across Cleveland's racial lines. The move to Lee-Harvard was my second encounter with Cleveland's odd racial geography as well as its politics concerning race and education. Lee-Harvard's Charles Eliot had no Major Work classes, so after graduating from Boulevard in the sixth grade, I was forced to attend Alexander Hamilton, a junior high on the border of Mount Pleasant. Every morning I took two buses to return to the neighborhood that my parents had so eagerly escaped. There I saw my Robert Fulton classmates from whom I had been separated when I left for Boulevard. It was an odd homecoming.

This oddness reflected an irony that my parents discussed continually at dinner. They had departed Mount Pleasant as it filled with black newcomers from the inner city. When my mother and father arrived in Cleveland in 1947, both the eastern European immigrants and the black middle class were leaving the southeast side. The whites went to the new suburbs rapidly emerging on the southwest and southeast sides of Cleveland. The blacks went to formerly middle-class white neighborhoods—Lee-Harvard and Milverton—on the city's southeastern borders. From there, they would a few years later go back toward the city to Shaker Heights and Cleveland Heights. As the black bourgeoisie and white immigrants left neighborhoods such as Lee-Harvard, they left a wasteland in their wake. The houses in their old neighborhoods were sold, nevertheless, at inflated prices to the most desperate and ambitious inner-city patrons of Cleveland's choked Negro real estate market. These inflated prices only provided further incentive for the remaining whites to sell their homes.

The city's mayor came to Lee-Harvard during the neighborhood's crisis and was confronted by a crowd of angry whites resisting the presence of blacks in their neighborhood. Whites clearly feared the erosion of property values. My parents talked endlessly about the brokers, their realty companies, and the media coverage of the crisis surrounding integration. And the newspapers, which I was then beginning to read, discussed it with equal passion. Acutely aware of Cleveland's racial atmosphere, my parents had never suspected the papers of making benevolent gestures to black people. However, even writers for the *Cleveland Press* were bothered by the notion of tampering with the region's fundamental democratic promise: social mobility and neighborhood comfort for all. At the heart of Cleveland's attraction was the promise of the suburbs, which were widely assumed to be the birthright of every Clevelander. What did it mean for this promise to be sold and then devalued? This question was striking enough that even a racist press felt compelled to consider it in relation to blacks from the city. For my parents, of course, this devaluation of their dreams had even deeper effects. What they had worked for all their lives was now to be blown up and burst like one of the cheap penny balloons that the tellers at the Society National Bank passed out to children on Fridays. What did these policies signify about the value of their middle-class aspirations? My parents had left segregation in the South only to encounter a more mobile and flexible version of Jim Crow in the North. This point, of course, was a universal truism in the city and raised a philosophical question that every aspiring black Clevelander had to consider.

In the early eighties, I married a woman from South Carolina whose brother had come to Cleveland in the 1970s and made the long trek to Warrensville Heights, the eastern suburb south of Lee-Harvard. He was part of a later intra-city black migration, which eventually extended deeper southward. He still lives there and works in a youth program with young black inner-city men on probation. He has refused to move farther into the suburbs despite his financial ability to do so. "If," he asks his charges, "you stand in the inner city and take the 32 line up Cedar Road through Cleveland Heights, through University Heights, through Beachwood, through Gates Mills, and finally arrive at the newest and richest development on Cleveland's suburban frontier, will you be any different than when you first got on the bus?" Since its foundation, the city had posed this question to all its striving immigrants, whether they came from eastern Europe or from the black rural South. The question epitomizes an American conundrum too—a problem that a young black Emerson might have raised had he lived in Mount Pleasant in 1962. My brother-in-law's simple question inquires into the ultimate possibilities of the New World. What would America be if the frontier were routinely transformed into the site from which one just departed, if movement brought about no change, if one's immediate social world were always on the verge of being frozen into tradition?

By the time we moved to Lee-Harvard, a number of blacks were already there. Indeed the arrival of any black in a Cleveland neighborhood, my mother would eventually observe sarcastically, was an omen that the whole neighborhood would eventually darken. Walking down the street on Saturday mornings, I noticed groups of thirteen-, fourteen-, and fifteen-year-old black boys. They wore jeans and ragged T-shirts and walked with the slight swagger then called the "pimp walk." One of them usually carried a transistor radio from which an R&B tune blared. Their long steps and swinging arms announced their angry possession of their surroundings. I would often hear them say that they would not tolerate the presence of any white boys, meaning the largely WASP population across the nearby border between Shaker Heights and the northern side of Lee-Harvard.

As whites fled the movement of blacks into Lee-Harvard, blacks had discovered the extent of their exclusion from Cleveland's white Polish, Hungarian, German, and Czech world. That knowledge, more than any black separatist ideology, made the black boys angry, and they were determined to possess—if only in appearance—the streets that they patrolled in groups. They glared at me, already recognizing me as a newcomer to their world. Would I join them, they seemed to be asking, or was I chicken shit? I looked back at them, recognized their anger as the rage that had welled up within me in the Boulevard classroom, and was horrified.

At Alexander Hamilton Junior High School, the teachers barely went through the motions of the most banal communication with their black students. Cleveland's cohort of ethnic teachers who had earlier feared the possibility of a black majority now looked upon that dark presence with outright despair. The most proficient of my classmates simply mastered the art of completing meaningless assignments. There were only a few exceptions to this rule. I remained in the special classes for gifted students, and I had good teachers in math and French. Mildred Brady, a superb French teacher, was my first black literature teacher—an attractive, slender, smart woman in her fifties whom I saw during my summertime French courses at Western Reserve University, where she was a graduate student of Romance languages.

Short and brown skinned, she energetically and persuasively taught Racine to a group of increasingly jaded advanced black students who were finding it easier to laugh at rather than with Racine. She liked to speak a few words of Italian with the Italians who remained in such classes. The great masses of black children from the surrounding elementary schools, including many who had gone to Fulton, were strangers to me. They were, I now realize, the newcomers from the urban ghetto in the central city who had displaced the middle class now moving farther east, south, and sometimes north from Mount Pleasant. At Alexander Hamilton, I observed groups of young black boys similar to those who patrolled the Lee-Harvard streets on Saturday mornings. These youths gathered outside the classroom before and after class and mobbed the halls between class periods. Policemen in dark-blue uniforms walked conspicuously to the principal's office, and in their wake, mobs now and again would erupt in excitement or anger. These volatile young people surrounded me in homeroom, where I began my school day. Many of these students had repeated seventh grade more than once. "There are a lot of old niggers here," they would cynically joke while loitering in the halls before school began.

My grades had begun to tail off when I first arrived at Boulevard. I had gotten straight A's in the sixth grade. Now at Alexander Hamilton, my academic performance, never stable, deteriorated once more. I had considered myself, despite my shortcomings, to be intellectually exceptional, and here again I found my uniqueness failing when put to the test. We were seated in Mr. Pfeifer's math and algebra classes in rows according to our course averages. It was a compelling way of encouraging class achievement, but I found myself among the very worst performers in the class, in no way competing—despite my arrogance—with those students who were quickly becoming accepted as the best. This was the most concrete possible evidence of my mediocrity. As

I fell over the next year to the bottom of my eighth-grade algebra class, my earlier, more hopeful self-conception seemed to mock me. For I was indistinguishable from those considered goof-offs, even by the standards of the classroom's middling students. It is no surprise that I spent more and more of my time gazing at the long, stockinged legs of my classmate Evelyn Nowacki. As my grades continued to decline in the eighth and ninth grades, I realized my academic kinship to the class's lowliest students and finally broke away from the routines of school life in my own way.

At some point near the end of the seventh grade, I dawdled to the bus stop; realized I was already late for school; and, in a spontaneous exercise of will, decided to cut class. Drifting around Lee-Harvard, I caught the 56a at a stop much farther ahead than usual. I was surprised at how empty the bus was. Apparently the 7:15 bus that I caught was a rush-hour run. I got off at 135th and Corlett. Enlivened by my daring, I walked into the Hungarian bakery there and bought a Danish pastry, paying the suspicious woman who silently took my money and turned away with a look of revulsion. I don't think that she spoke much English. Her equally bad-tempered sister, with whom she ran the store, probably handled much of its business. They did not like the black teenagers who drifted in while waiting for the bus. Stragglers in small crowds routinely entered the shop and stole from the window display when the sliding glass doors were open at both ends. Occasionally the police were called. Remembering this, I became alarmed and hurried out of the shop. I rushed to school and entered the guidance office to face the consequences of my tardiness. Upon giving a confected excuse, I was allowed to proceed unscathed to class. I had never been late before. So common was this minor truancy at Alexander Hamilton that detention was required only for repeat offenders.

Like many a socially incompetent, bookish boy, I immersed myself in literature in response to the disruptions of puberty. One of my teachers, Mr. Vargo, was a large, somnolent, red-faced man who had apparently given up on serious instruction. He once made a joke in the sexual language of the street—a reference to rapping and daddy rap. He was as useless a teacher as I was a student. I remember none of the stories we read that semester, nor the papers we wrote. But over the course of the term, he used texts from an anthology that contained several poems by Robert Frost; these interested me greatly, and I memorized a number of them. Two were "Stopping by Woods on a Snowy Evening" and "Dust of Snow."

I immediately saw that Frost's verse demonstrated the distracted, inward-looking manner to which I had drifted since discovering *Grimm's Fairy Tales*, science fiction, and the biblical stories of our church's simple Sunday school books. Discovering his poetry, I found a means of placing the large imaginative spaces of the art museum, the dance floor, and Boulevard's Major Work classroom within myself. Frost's drowsy way of looking at the world could yield marvelous realms of internal feeling. And I felt these feelings emerge in his imagined accounts of a horse's thoughts, a snow shower's transformation of mood, and an observer's moment of silent communication with a colt. Here was a poet who quite obviously had discovered such dreaming inclinations in himself, who specialized in discovering the truths revealed in such reverie.

All daydreamers wish for some social authority to validate their private intuitions. I therefore took Frost's poetry as a great gift. I spent much of my Saturday mornings being scolded by my father for woolgathering in our backyard in Lee-Harvard, and here was a distinguished poet whose power in verses such as "Two Tramps in Mud Time" and "After Apple-Picking" flowed from such meditative sleepwalking in print. At any rate, I had little chance to do anything but dream because of the changes in my body. Too distracted by my own sexual excitement and endless daydreaming, I could not keep track of the equations written by my slender blonde algebra teacher on the blackboard. My attention might be totally arrested by a girl's partially unbuttoned blouse, the shape of her hips, or the lift of her breast as she yawned, stretching her back, each erotic display causing my moment-by-moment identity to dislocate, and eventually my very selfhood to disintegrate. My body seemed less an extension of my nervous system and more a subterranean disturbance, the site of sudden change that shook me without warning.

My father addressed this change in his usual sly manner. When I attended Dalcroze lessons at the Cleveland settlement house in the third and fourth grades, he had spoken to me, half seriously, half mockingly, about white girls. Did I like the young white girls with whom I danced at Dalcroze on Saturdays at the settlement house? he asked. In rural Kentucky, he continued, boys my age had been lynched for looking at such girls. At Kentucky State, young white women called out to neatly dressed black male students on their way to class. At night mixed-race couples would meet amid the bushes to tryst and flirt under cover of darkness. As I began junior high, he revived this mode of joking. "Are you going to marry that girl?" he asked, referring to the girl I liked in Dalcroze. "You said that you were going to marry that girl." In an equally bland tone, he might describe the male sexual impulse as an insanity that drove men out of control and to their own destruction. I had never been driven out of my mind by the girl in Dalcroze, yet I reflected that, given the chance, now I might.

My confusion deepened as my father warned me about sex while we tended the lawn on late Saturday afternoons. He was a custodian in inner-city schools, and my mother had begun to encounter the explosive world of Hough and Glenville now displaced to the Murray Hill border of the city's southeastern periphery at the nursery school in University Circle where she was a teacher. The inner-city world of which these children were a part frightened both my parents, but particularly, to my surprise, my father. If sex could be the source of pleasure, it was also at the center of the disintegrating urban ghetto as a crazed masculine rage drove students to vandalize schools, ripping thermostats from the wall, and stealing speakers and other electrical equipment. All this made my father angry in a way that could lead him to condemn the city's seemingly oceanic black erotic force as it rumbled like an earthquake. He expressed his disgust with this disorder harshly. Seemingly a propos of nothing, he once commented that he would rather go to the electric chair than raise a sexually promiscuous child. Although these warnings kept me from speaking to girls in any but the most formal way, they could not control my dreams. Night after night, I dreamed of being strapped into the death instrument only to be reprieved at the last minute before waking.

My classmates were at that moment discovering sex among the prostitutes on Kinsman. Erotic thoughts possessed them as ruthlessly as they did me. Their experience was not vicarious, although their accounts were as vivid as my dreams. In the shower and locker rooms, amid the odd male intimacy produced by shared nudity, these young people said many remarkable things. One, a tall slender boy of nearly seventeen, recounted his solicitation of a girl on the street that morning: "If she had a dick, I asked her, would she fuck herself?" I would never give voice to my fantasies in public, but they were at least as shocking and contorted.

Insisting that I continue to dress in plain chinos, blue oxford shirts, and loafers even as my classmates began to flaunt the flashy adornment displayed in the windows of the stores that had sprung up around Kinsman, my parents perhaps understood my emerging feelings far too well. As we trimmed the shrubbery in our yard one Saturday afternoon, my father told me that sexual desire was an uncontrollable impulse. When he said this, I realized that my classmates dancing in the school hallways, the toughs pimping down 140th

Street, and the whores strolling in front of the bars on Kinsman were all caught up in this frenzy. For the first time, it seemed strangely inviting. Why was I so good? What, given the chance, might I myself not do?

At my parents' insistence—they were deeply worried by my academic decline—I became a paperboy for the *Cleveland Plain Dealer*. They sought to impose some discipline in my life. The new job, however, only opened another sphere to my meandering observation of the world. As I made collections for my paper route on Fridays and Saturdays, I heard R&B tunes through my customers' screen doors. Women came to pay their bills dressed only in pajamas. The world of the street seen house to house on Invermere was, with its black leather coats and silk ghetto finery, like a circus of risk-defying daredevils and acrobats. The music flaunted expressiveness suggesting both familiarity and contempt. As Cleveland's East Side became black and the city's population tilted toward a Negro majority, it was impossible to hear this music and not connect it with the antics of George Forbes, the sly, politically astute, and flamboyant councilman who insulted his white colleagues, city judges, TV cameramen, and reporters with no apologies.

I could not dissociate myself from these changes. One day at school, unable to open my locker door, I called for help. The squat white assistant principal, Mr. Yuhass, finally appeared and instructed me to help him pull open the door. We eventually succeeded, pulling with all our might. When we were done, he delivered an insult that seemed to come out of nowhere. Puffing and sweaty, he demanded to know why I could not open the door by myself. "What's the matter with you?" he asked. "Are you a faggot?"

I said nothing, shocked. After a minute or so, I was able to sort things out. It was a telling question, however rhetorical. He used the word "faggot" to refer not to homosexuality but to my weakness, and also as racial taunt. Was I not, Mr. Yuhass was asking, one of those tough niggers who confronted him in the hallway on a daily basis? Such Negroes were now the stock-in-trade of soul music and the dancehalls. Was I a fag? *American Bandstand* was, of course, at that time asking Mr. Yuhass whether he and white middle-class schoolteachers like him were not fags. He had no answer to this question and had fallen into impotent rage.

Near the end of the semester, depressed by my algebra grade, I drifted to the 56A bus stop and decided to cut school again. The leaves in the trees of Mount Pleasant were bright. The grass, however, was littered with loose paper wrappers, liquor bottles, and cigarette butts. Nearing the school, I considered the eighteen- and nineteen-year-olds lingering around the entrance to the school, many of whom had spent as many as five and six years at a three-year junior high, and I promised myself never to cut school again. There was nothing in this world, it was now clear, of interest to me. This cut, however, was my second of the year, and the counselor in the office assigned me to detention that evening.

Familiar though I was with the crowds that daily occupied the cafeteria at noon, the front halls in the morning, and the schoolyard in the evening, I was not prepared for the large black mass I saw after school during detention: a shiny black-surfaced human sea rippled before me, taut with its own internal being. It seemed at first that I had never seen so many young black people together in one room. On the stage at the front of the auditorium stood Mr. Morton, a tall, broad-shouldered black teacher. He had a long wooden paddle that he held by his side as he surveyed the auditorium. From time to time, he would pick out a particularly visible offender and direct him to the stage, where he was publicly swatted before the assembly. After a while this spectacle went unnoticed, the crowd having assumed a life of its own.

I watched this scene with increasing disbelief. This was the kind of picture of hell that I might see in a comic book. Mr. Morton selected one victim after another, impressively shellacking each one's rump. The victims showed little or no dismay or contrition. The crowd in the auditorium went on surging and swaying, oblivious to the punitive ritual onstage, moving to its own rhythms.

I had never had Mr. Morton as a teacher. He was well dressed, favoring the kind of brown suits, tastefully matching ties, and cordovan shoes that I associated with church wear. He wore a neatly trimmed moustache, and he clearly spent some time picking out his ties. His concern with his appearance extended to his credibility on the street. I had him pegged as an overbearing male teacher who gloried in his reputation for paddling, and I suspect that my tougher black classmates had his number too. Because he seemed so concerned with his image, he could be easily intimidated by the threat of violence. I had sometime earlier seen him in the cafeteria arguing with a group of boys gathered in a mob against a wall. This must have been 1964. Cassius Clay—not yet Mohammad Ali—had just beaten Sonny Liston for the first time, and the boys waved in Morton's face a newspaper picture of the triumphant Clay gesturing to the crowd as he leaned against the ropes. Excited by the picture of the shouting, victorious Clay, the boys attempted to draw Morton's attention to the picture. The boastful Ali had become their hero, and they were now shoving him in Morton's face. As they argued, a crowd of students swelled and pressed upon the teacher. Morton grew quiet, suddenly aware of his own vulnerability. As he was about to respond, his mouth closed, and his face went slack. The next moment he quickly left the room with his partially filled tray.

Remembering this event, I watched Mr. Morton onstage with greater interest. I was only awakened from my spell when I saw him pointing at me. I shook my head in disbelief. From the stage he nodded yes. Now aware of his distance from me, I paused for a moment. A disturbance—two quarrelling girls in a scuffle—started up on the other side of the auditorium. Suddenly the bell signaling the end of detention rang. I walked quickly into the school hallway and was swallowed up by the exiting mob. Looking back, I saw Mr. Morton standing alone on the stage.

After receiving a D in algebra, I had to repeat the course that summer in order to stay in Major Work. Unexpectedly, I encountered a marvelous black math teacher at Adams High School. My math probably also improved because I read the book over and over again, but I cannot separate my newfound energy from this teacher who not only caught my attention in class but inspired me to complete my assignments as soon as I got home.

I remained, however, angry in a free-floating way and often directed my rage at whatever was disturbing me at the moment. My ire, whatever its force, had never goaded me to action, but near the end of the summer semester, a particularly large swarm of blacks outside the Hungarian bakery did. Like me, they had come from summer school at John Adams to idle around the small Hungarian bakery. The two elderly proprietors usually communicated with their young black customers through a combination of gestures and grunts. The crowd that day was particularly alive, swirling with the internal energy I had first seen in the school auditorium during detention. At some point in their exchange with the women, the black youths took offense, and in the midst of this confrontation, a tall youth wearing a silk shirt barked a command for the largest cake on the far corner of a shelf facing the display window. Implausible as the sincerity of his request seemed—what did a sixteen-year-old need with a four-layer cake?—the nervous women found themselves stymied. The woman nearest the designated cake slid one of the case's interior doors open, carelessly leaving the opposite end of the display window uncovered. Distracted by the growing crowd, her sister leaned against the wall, waiting for the students to leave.

The sisters were usually alert to the dangers of an unintentional opening of the display window. Stealing was common, and given the black presence at this bus stop around this time each day, the police answered calls quickly. Innocent bystanders were often nabbed in situations such as this and driven away in the squad car. Such an offense was not necessarily a trifling matter in the Cleveland juvenile courts. A conviction might, the word at Hamilton was, lead to six months in reform school; a second rap might mean even worse.

Emboldened by the nervousness of the women, the young people nearest the far end of the window began to pocket pastries from the array of buns, cakes, tarts, and pies on display. The window opened further as the crowd in the store grew, and what was initially pilfering became a spree. I ran out of the store into the waiting 56a bus. Seeing the melee, the bus driver had parked his vehicle at the curb and called the police. From the bus window, I watched. I could now see the inner display window lean and sway under the students' weight. Two policemen arrived only to find themselves inadequate to the task of controlling the mob. Suddenly four more squad cars appeared. The display case was now empty, and the women were nowhere to be seen. I was getting hungry, and somewhere, I idly thought, was that huge multilayered cake, probably split into pieces. The drama now apparently over, a large crowd of students entered the bus. The policemen stood around the front of the shop, unsure of their next move.

Finally the two frustrated policemen stormed the bus, apparently motivated by their embarrassment. However, some students on the bus now sensed they had the upper hand. As the two white cops walked to the back, they accidentally brushed the new yellow calfskin shoes of an arrogant light-skinned boy who lived across the street from me on Invermere. "Don't they teach you cops any manners?" he yelled. "You get off the bus!" one of policemen ordered, and they took him out.

They were greeted by the remnants of the mob, still giddy from its triumph over the shopkeepers. As the policemen paused on the sidewalk, the young blacks surrounded them. A conflict with the outnumbered cops was in the offing, and the crowd tensed with anticipation. Would the policemen act, or were they scared? The policemen talked to the boy and sternly guided him back to the bus, one of them walking alongside him, the other following him. On the bus, the first cop was greeted with howls of laughter. "You stupid motherfucker!" a voice called as the policemen turned to leave. Both policemen looked around, unable to distinguish the speaker from among the hive of black visages before them. Both officers now sternly gazed at the crowd, turned again, and prepared to leave. "Faggots!" I yelled after they'd turned. Not bothering to look this time, the cops shrugged their shoulders and left the bus. The crowd outside had drifted away, and the two policemen drove off.

CHAPTER FIVE

Antioch Baptist Church
and the Emmers

Settling in Cleveland, my parents, like most blacks recently up from the South, spent some time seeking a church. For a while they visited East Mount Zion, far up on 107th Street. Although my mother's skin color, her education, and her connection with Park Synagogue qualified her for this upper-class congregation of doctors, lawyers, and established civil servants, my father's job as a custodian and his lack of prospects made him suited only for the storefronts. Then they attended St. James Church on 91st and Cedar. Finally they settled upon Antioch Baptist Church on 89th and Cedar, a middle-class congregation founded by black migrants to the city in the twenties and already well established by the late thirties. When we came to Antioch, it was Cleveland's largest black church.

At the head of the church was the Reverend Wade McKinney, a portly, light-skinned figure. One of Cleveland's major civic leaders, he represented the rising place of blacks in a still highly segregated Cleveland in the late fifties and early sixties. The son of a sharecropper and a product of the turn-of-the-century migration, he had left Mississippi for the North in the teens. He graduated from Morehouse College and later Colgate Rochester Divinity School, where he wrote a thesis on the role of the church in northern migration. In Cleveland, he was instrumental in founding Forest City Hospital, for a long time the only black hospital. He consistently spoke out against segregation in employment and housing and was active in voting drives. He was also the first black foreman of the Cuyahoga County Grand Jury. Other church members were also conspicuously successful. Dr. Toney, an orthodontist, served as clinical professor at Western Reserve Dental School, and Dr. Turner, a professor at

Reserve's school of social work, would eventually become dean of the school and later a professor at Chapel Hill.

My parents found themselves at sea amid the Byzantine hierarchy of deacon boards, ladies auxiliaries, and various other clubs and organizations of Antioch. Unlikely people often rose within the complicated politics of Antioch's church life. One of the head deacons, a short, dignified, ruddy-faced man who stood immediately outside the sanctuary shaking the hands of the important folk of the church, was a longtime member. After school, I would see him riding the No. 14 bus up Kinsman. Apparently a workman at a kiln or brickyard or shop, he wore a blue work uniform coated in yellow dust.

Over the course of his long career at Antioch, McKinney, by the time he met our family, had seen many Cleveland Negroes of all ranks, shapes, and types pass through his church. He had obviously picked out those who were already successes or those who were bound to succeed. An important activist in the black migrants' early days, he was now not just a go-between linking the city's white establishment to the masses but also part of Cleveland's colored elite. Indeed, he was one of the elite's gatekeepers. He clearly saw my mother, whom he greeted warmly, as possessing the potential to enter this elite; however, my father could not have cut much of a figure in Rev. McKinney's eyes.

During services my parents sat erect, their faces emotionless, and required me and my squirming young brother and sisters to do the same. There were times at Antioch when it was impossible to ignore our lowly place in the congregation. There was a hierarchy of four cadres of men who helped serve bread and wine, as well as collecting the Communion offering. The first group, the deacons, stood around the Communion table. The second, a subset of the first, served Communion. A third group took up the empty glasses. And a fourth group took a collection after Communion. The members of the first two groups wore white gloves; the men in the second two did not. My father belonged to the very last group. By the time he and his fellows took up the last of the church's three daily Communion offerings, only loose change appeared in the felt-bottomed wooden bowl. He never garnered Rev. McKinney's approval and complained about it at home after church. Clarence Richards reciprocated McKinney's perceived snubs by falling asleep—his eyes deceitfully open—as the minister gave his wordy weekly sermons.

During the distribution of bread and grape juice, there was some singing, and when the choir had finished, the organist played slow, sad spirituals while the audience hummed. The playing and humming continued for nearly twenty minutes until the last group made the final pass through the congregation. The humming during Communion moved me more than anything else at church. It was the kind of thing that the genteel McKinney despised. He, to my parents' approval, sharply forbade the customary response of "Amen" and "That's right" to the music and to his preaching. Indeed, he would often tell those who did respond in such a way to be quiet.

My parents disapproved of this humming also, and neither ever joined in it. At the dinner table, they could be very adamant about this; they had come to the North, they said, to find nothing but the moaning of black people. From where I sat, however, self-pitying moans were a more than appropriate response to the experience of black people in Cleveland. On the No. 48 bus going to French class in the summer, I had on Fridays seen the black maids coming home from their weekly stints with their white employers on Van Aken, on South Park, and from points east. On those days, they carried large brown shopping bags from the suburban supermarket, Heinens, filled with leftover food and their employers' cast-off dresses and skirts. No matter who these black women had been in the South, they were now servants in Cleveland. It occurred to me then that the post-Communion music expressed wordlessly everything they could never say to their employers in the mansions of Shaker Heights. The deepest truth about Cleveland that I was learning from my family was that Cleveland's racial truths could never be openly discussed, at least not in public by people like me. If being black, however, meant that one carried a wordless secret truth, then I would willingly be black. Why, I wondered a little angrily, did my parents not hum?

I experienced baptism by immersion in the church's blue-tiled font and believed in God as an omnipresent spirit who oversaw my life and everything else. I acquired this deep belief from my parents, who prayed sincerely before meals and, in junior church, offered Bible verses when they were called upon to do so by Rev. McKinney's buxom wife. They searched, however, for something else. Despite their focused energies and plans, they were troubled. They seemed after a while to take the racism of the school board and the city's municipal administration for granted, but they were, as the years went by, increasingly concerned for their children. Despite my evident academic promise, my grades and moods were erratic, my sister Patrice's more so. My younger sister showed little interest in school. When we were angry, the older of my two sisters and I could be a rebellious, disruptive force.

Both of my parents had been raised in southern black Baptist families. They were not medical people, and perhaps for this reason, they—unlike my Aunt Gladys, a nurse—turned to therapy only later in life. They, perhaps predictably, turned to religion. This development, as well as their desire to participate in the Antioch community, led them to seek a solution to family problems in prayer. The Nomads, a group of young families, discussed problems related to marriage and child-rearing on Sunday afternoons and evenings. As their name suggested, they felt themselves to be wandering in Cleveland's urban wilderness. Three or four hours after church, Mom and Dad would participate in this group's meetings. Together this group decided to confront the issues that faced them through prayer in what was, in fact, informal revival. I do not know how the group made this decision, but it was consistent with the church's practice of prayer, Bible reading, and discussing the religious meanings of one's daily experience in the language of the church.

The Nomads program included not only group prayer on Sunday afternoons but also weekday family prayers, a ritual with which my family experimented for three or four weeks. These sessions were rigid and forced, marked not by open expression of religious feeling but by painful self-restraint and formality. I remember them particularly because we kneeled for prayer, each facing a chair. As I closed my eyes, I had my first real experience of religious doubt. Kneeling on the gray carpet of our living room, I felt nothing, nothing at all.

My parents and other group members may have had a similar experience, for soon afterward they abandoned this ritual. They next threw themselves into a campaign to sell candy to offset the church's bills. The church contacted a candy vendor, and my parents committed themselves to selling the eight or ten cans of chocolate-covered pecans that they brought home with them one Sunday evening from a Nomads meeting.

To my older sister and me, the candy was a powerful but challenging temptation. The cans were sealed with a removable metal strip just below the top rim. One opened the candy by twisting the container's flexible metal strip with a key glued to the top of the can. One closed the whole thing by fitting the can's top, now narrower without the strip, back on. We were at first stumped by this device and decided we needed a more substantial amount of time to defeat it. Thus, we did not attempt to get at the candy until the next Nomads meeting. Unable to manipulate the key cleanly, however, both of us cut our fingers on the sharp metal strip that sprang out of the coil as we tried to roll it up.

Our grandmother's sudden appearance complicated this predicament. Outraged by the mess of blood, metal, and chocolate-covered pecans on the floor, she pointed to both of us and demanded that we go to our rooms. We rebelled instead, running upstairs to the attic. Having reached the top of the stairwell, we looked back down to our grandmother. She had followed us as far as the second-floor landing, upset that we had not gone to our rooms to take our punishment. Increasingly nervous as we anticipated our parents' return from the meeting, we soon became fearful. In the heat of our confusion, we took what we felt to be the only course of action available to us: frightening our grandmother away from the bottom of the stairwell. To do so, we removed a drawer from an old chest in the attic and dropped it directly down the stairwell to the landing, where my grandmother stood. The drawer shattered when it hit the floor. We did not see our grandmother for the rest of the night, until we returned downstairs to clean up the bloody mess, where our parents found us when they returned from the Nomads meeting.

After surveying the bloody candy container and the partially emptied cardboard box on the floor, our parents bathed us and put us to bed. And that Monday afternoon, I saw them relaxed for what seemed to be the first time in recent memory. The release of my anger and that of my sister seemed to lessen the tension in the house. Although they did not mention the incident when we came home from school, they also did not make us practice the piano, clean our rooms, hang up our clothes, or attend to our chores. We were as if magically relieved. And they were relieved too. They suspended any further discussion of their worries about us, at least in our presence, for months. They occasionally skipped church to sleep in. For a brief time, they seemed happy to forget whatever burden they had been carrying.

A new friend and his parents gave me an important new perspective on life when I was fifteen years old. Darwin Jackson Jr., his father, and his mother seemed at every turn to contest my assumptions about life. During the eighth grade at Alexander Hamilton, Darwin entered my class from a section of Major Work in Collinwood, a school on the ghetto's eastern fringes. I often went to his house to play ping-pong following school. Afterward, his father would drive me home. It was a short distance, only about three-quarters of a mile, but he had a great deal to say to me in that brief time. Both Mr. Jackson and his wife were smart people, social workers who had met while preparing for their German language examination as graduate students at Western Reserve University's school of social work. They had been raised in urban Cleveland, and Darwin's father taught our Sunday school class.

Mr. Jackson shunned the stuffy dress, formal tones, and stiff bearing of the teachers, dentists, and lawyers at Antioch. At some point the deacons at Antioch refused to allow a funeral for a Jackson relative at the church, angering the Jacksons, who saw it as a snub. A short man with a small belly, Mr. Jackson often wore a sweater and plaid shirts when teaching Sunday school. He spoke with the aggressive force of the young men pimping up and down Invermere. They walked with an ease that made them appear to glide. At Sunday school and at home, he rarely failed to respond to any observation by putting an interesting spin on it and posing questions I could not answer.

Early in his life, Darwin Jr. had had a kidney removed. Soon after we met, he told me that he lived with the knowledge that, barring the unlikely appearance of a donated kidney, the loss of his other kidney would mean his death. He told me this in a serious way that demonstrated his mature acceptance of the limitations of life. Despite his quite normal boyish interests in ping-pong, bowling, and girls, Darwin and his father and mother already had a sense of what one might call higher concerns. These concerns differed from my mother's pursuit of culture; indeed, they focused on living life to the fullest, and this meant living fully in the black world surrounding them. Their family was in no rush to move to the most recently integrated section of Shaker or Cleveland Heights. They knew that their presence there could ignite the short fuse of blockbusting if in fact their move was not part of an intra-city black migration already underway. The Jacksons brought a thoughtful outlook to what my mother described as the black community's casual acceptance of flashy dress and concern with the changing fashions in the R&B music played on the radio, as well as the illegal activities of the ghetto. The Jacksons accepted the black hustlers and pimps, the shopkeepers who fenced their goods, and the lawyers who defended them from the white world run from Shaker Heights, Rocky River, and Parma by white Ivy League businessmen, Italian judges, and Polish cops. It was no accident that the Jacksons, both of whom had studied sociology on their way to becoming social workers, had master's degrees in their field. They brought a calm, rational detachment to their understanding of the city's fast-and-loose ways.

Mr. Jackson's observations were too shrewd to be ignored, at least by me, and my mother and father discussed them with grim admiration, suspicion, and uneasiness. My mother considered the Jacksons part of the city despite their professional connection to the world of University Circle, where I took music and French lessons with white children from the suburbs. My parents kept a close eye on my relationship with Darwin and his father. The leather coats and expensive automobiles possessed by the Jacksons and the presence of alcohol in their home signified to my parents a wayward consumption of luxury goods typical of the ghetto world. My mother and father disapproved of the fact that the Jacksons had lived in a duplex in the declining Collinwood neighborhood for such a long time. My parents experienced discomfort at the ease with which the Jacksons had assimilated into the ways of black city life.

I remember one particular incident from Mr. Jackson's Sunday school classes. He liked to use examples from everyday life when he talked about ethics. He conceived of morality in terms of the daily decisions one made about one's friends, hobbies, and family. At some point, he discussed a decision he had made as a social worker during the past week. He had been chosen by a group of his colleagues to participate in a committee that made up the lists of patients to whom the hospital would offer dialysis treatment but chose to decline the honor.

As in many of Mr. Jackson's stories, there was a buried moral in this one. Although I was shocked by his decision to reject what was clearly an honor bestowed upon him by colleagues who were apparently mostly white, I could not, as my parents did, simply attribute his decision to his pessimism about the impossibility of significantly improved race relations. I could only partially grasp this at the time, but Mr. Jackson was making a statement about his relationship to white people in America. Why should he be held responsible for life-and-death decisions in a society that discriminated so ruthlessly against black people far less advantaged and lucky than he? Indeed, in what sense was he himself a member of that society? And why should he behave as if he were a member? As I remember this incident, I realize that he was laying it on the line for me as he was laying it on the line for his white colleagues even less disposed to understand him.

These views had much to do with his contempt for the integrationist movement, a contempt fueled by a militancy that was before its time. My parents were integrationists who, as the civil rights movement heated up in Cleveland, participated in interracial discussion groups with white suburbanites who drove in from Cleveland or Shaker Heights to talk to Negroes. On weekend evenings they dressed up—my father in a dark blue suit, my mother in a starched white blouse and a plain dark-blue skirt to go to these meetings. His father, my friend Darwin told me, knew of this project but would have no part of it. What, I could imagine Mr. Jackson snorting, was there to discuss that any white or black Cleveland adult did not already know, whatever he or she claimed?

Mr. Jackson's shrewd intelligence and his way of life allowed him to openly express his anger about the racial and political matters that my parents quietly

referred to as the affairs·of "our people" and "the other group." He had apparently sorted out and reflected upon the dangers of the repression of such anger.
Loudly and in public, he held forth on such things that my parents discussed in
the privacy of their bedrooms or indirectly at the dinner table. Significantly, the
Jackson family openly displayed all sorts of anger in their household. On one of
the coffee tables in their living room was a miniature doghouse with four tiny
dogs, each representing a member of the Jackson family. Each week a particular
dog was placed in the doghouse to indicate the family's general displeasure with
the person represented by that figurine. Occasionally Mr. Jackson's figurine ended
up in the doghouse. Nothing was hidden in that house. Given Mr. Jackson's
politics, I was not surprised when Darwin Jr. reported that his father liked to
recount the story of a racial insult he had experienced as a college student. On
his way to Wilberforce, the bus operator addressed young Mr. Jackson as "boy."
Feeling that he might take the operator by surprise, Mr. Jackson had responded,
"Who the hell are you calling 'boy'?" This was the kind of expression of anger
that—from what I could make out—did not fly with white people in Cleveland
and explained Mr. Jackson's attitude toward the discussion groups that my parents
participated in. "Why should I put on a suit to sit in white folks' living rooms
when I wear a hunting shirt to church?" I could hear Mr. Jackson asking.

We as a family in the early sixties seemed to enter the living rooms of the white
folks on exactly those terms that Mr. Jackson distained. I recall the Emmers as
my parents' closest friends during the early to mid-sixties, when I entered my
teens. A Jewish family, they lived on a leafy Cleveland Heights street near the
intersection of Mayfield and Lee. They had been leftists during the late forties
and early fifties and persisted with their radical views in somewhat the same
way that Mr. Jackson persisted in a militant separatism. Jack was a social worker
who was involved in the reconciliation of conflicts among black militants, local
Cleveland political leaders, and the shopkeeper community during the sixties,
and Ruth taught nursery school with my mother at Park. Toby, their daughter,
was about sixteen, and their son Howie a year or so younger. Ruth was chatty and
quick. Jack spoke slowly and deliberately with a sadness that reminded me of the
humming during Communion at Antioch Baptist Church. Their conversations
with my parents seemed to be full of significance. They called them Clarence and
Juanita as if they were good friends who had been through a sad time together.

Jack and Ruth were very gracious and generous people. I was particularly
amazed at their openness. I entered their house for the first time when they

invited our family to a Passover seder. I had never eaten gefilte fish before or tasted the panoply of ritual seder dishes. I felt welcome enough in their home to browse through their bookshelves and record collection. Their bookshelves—unlike ours, which held *Reader's Digest Condensed Books* and issues of *Reader's Digest* and *U.S. News and World Report*—were filled with many books, and in their record collection I found the recordings of Martha Schlamme, Pete Seeger, and the Weavers.

Ruth and Jack lived with a dignified simplicity that my mother in particular found attractive. The Emmers seemed comfortable. They drove small foreign cars. He dressed simply in jeans and sports shirts. The sofas and armchairs in their living room exuded ease but not luxuriousness, and no bottles of whisky, gin, or rum were conspicuously on display. Significantly they had suffered for their views. I quickly connected their simple lifestyles to their political connections. They had been blacklisted from jobs, and some of their friends had received prison sentences in connection with their leftist activities in the thirties and forties.

I was deeply impressed by the Emmers and the other Jewish intellectual radicals with whom they associated for other, more practical reasons. These concerned their immediate connection to our family. After refusing to be a day worker my mother had eventually become desperate for a job and willing to take work as a cleaning woman. The Jewish radicals had saved her from that humiliation, and she would, moreover, rise in the city's professional association of nursery schoolteachers on the basis of her job at Park. My parents' association with this group was, however, accompanied by some anomalies. To be sure, this world had connected my mother with important people such as the Ratners, who owned the Forest City Lumber Company; the pianist Eunice Podis; and the many successful doctors and academics she met at Park. From my mother's accounts, I sensed that these people lived a richer life than I. But I had no real contact with that life. One could not say that we knew them and their world in the way that my family knew the Jacksons and black Cleveland. However, my mother—and, to a lesser extent, my father—deferred to their authority as intellectuals who had thought seriously about politics and social commitment. My greatest impression of Park was that it was hidden by trees and bushes from my sight when my father and I stopped our car to pick my mother up from work. This may at times have given Jewish culture its inviting mystery, but it also created a boundary that no black could penetrate. I felt the presence of such a boundary in listening to the Emmers express their views.

༒

In the early sixties when my parents began visiting the Emmers, the activities of leftists, in particular alleged communists, were coming under the surveillance of the FBI. These leftists had already caught the attention of the Cleveland community during the trial of Fred and Marie Haug, whose daughter Lucy was my classmate at Alexander Hamilton. Both of the Haugs had been labor organizers in the late forties, and Marie Haug had run for a seat on the Cleveland Board of Education in the early fifties. The couple were, with others, charged with hiding their membership in the Communist Party. They were brought to trial, were convicted of conspiracy to defraud the government, and received relatively short prison sentences. Before their sentencing, the distinguished pediatrician Dr. Benjamin Spock testified that the simultaneous imprisonment of both parents would do irreversible psychological damage to their child, and Lucy's parents were therefore given staggered sentences. One parent remained out of jail to care for Lucy while the other served his or her prison term. Afterward, her mother entered graduate school in sociology at Western Reserve University and became a world-renowned sociologist, one of the intellectual founders and guiding lights of the field of gerontology. Some of the early articles that she wrote as a graduate student became classics in the discipline. She went on to become a distinguished professor and leader at Western Reserve University. Lucy would go on to become a physician.

At the time when we knew the Emmers in the early sixties, they were the subjects of allegations by the House Un-American Activities Committee. The communists were being connected with the infiltration of black political groups. FBI informers had tracked their movements and the social events that they held in their homes, and one such FBI informer, a black woman named Julia Brown, named the Emmers, implicitly accusing them of being communists by way of their association with other alleged communists. Marie Haug had been a victim of a similar attack as a result of her presence at a Paul Robeson concert in Cleveland.

The Emmers invited me to join the Student Peace Union, the peace group to which their children belonged. SPU hosted speakers from other peace groups such as the Committee for a Sane Nuclear Policy and the Fellowship for Reconciliation. I remember seeing the names of American intellectuals such as Seymour Lipset, Pitirim Sorokin, and Erich Fromm on the backs of pamphlets that I distributed in the wealthy sections of Cleveland Heights, where older women came to their doors and looked them over.

From the speakers who came to SPU meetings I heard about the leftist and civil rights activity in Cleveland as well as the world of socialist politics in eastern Europe, Cuba, and elsewhere in Latin America. The boys wore jeans and boots; the girls, sweaters and dark tights and skirts—the uniforms of the residual bohemian arts movement. They spoke of writing poetry and their own music and making art. I heard of the work of Paul Klee as well as the abstract expressionism of Jackson Pollock. I started going to the Cleveland Museum of Art. They spoke of Greenwich Village, Hyde Park in Chicago, and Berkeley, where their parents, many of whom seemed to be academics, had lectured.

The meetings' leftist critique continued after the conclusion of formal business. Taking out their shiny Gibson, Martin, and Goya guitars, members of the group played the songs by Phil Ochs and Tom Paxton most recently published in *Sing Out*. It was music of political protest that translated anger over injustice into dry wit.

William Worthy isn't worthy to enter our door
Went down to Cuba, he's not American anymore
But somehow it is strange to hear the State Department say
You are living in the free world, in the free world you must stay.[1]

These meetings appealed to me. The long-haired girls seated on couches or the floor speaking of classical music and poetry caught my attention. I found myself listening to political discussions while reflecting on the dreariness of my parents' lives in our Lee-Harvard home, cleaning the garage or shining shoes and ironing shirts for the next day's church service. I found myself sexually attracted to these girls and began to look into their faces and notice the casual way in which they looked at me. I was bothered by some elements of this political view. These included the dogmatic way in which they asserted their views on Cuba's autonomy and the improvements to eastern European life after the communist takeover. I was sometimes taken aback by the self-conscious way in which they wondered whether the Cleveland police had taken down their parents' license plate numbers when they were dropped off at the meetings. Indeed, when the House Un-American Activities Committee's reports were finally published, it became clear that their parents and other leftists were being followed at both

1. Phil Ochs, "Ballad of William Worthy," THE BALLAD OF WILLIAM WORTHY by Phil Ochs @1983 Chappell & Co. All Rights Reserved. Used by permission of Alfred Publishing Co., Inc.

formal and informal social events. However, the conversations of the parents—the Emmers and the Haugs—were free of this self-dramatizing quality.

My participation in SPU inevitably led me to participate in Student CORE, where I learned nonviolent tactics of protest from white organizers. The white teenagers from SPU served as organizers in Student CORE in much the same way their parents had been organizers and leaders in the labor unions of the forties and early fifties. Ready for the rigors of marches, sit-ins, and attacks by the cops, they dressed in T-shirts and jeans, the appropriate attire for learning to assume the fetal position in order to avoid damage to one's genitals and internal organs from a policeman's billy club. I felt out of place in the neatly pressed khakis and blue oxford shirts that my parents insisted I wear to the workshops. I was, unlike the others in the group, not eager to make an overt public display of my anger toward the city police.

I was always somewhat embarrassed by my parents' connection to the Emmers, whose casual clothes vividly contrasted with the slightly formal bearing of my parents. Despite their good will to my parents, patronage was patronage and implied a deference to white authority that I was beginning to find troubling. Status and authority, as my father hinted slyly and as Mr. Jackson proclaimed openly, were understood much differently by blacks than by the Jewish intellectuals my mother and I aspired to emulate.

On the other hand, there was an odd rightness in the relationship between my parents and the Emmers, who as leftists were also outsiders to most of the rest of the surrounding Jewish community and thus nonconformists somewhat in the manner of my parents. Their relationship represented an integrated style of life distinct from the racially segregated ethos of the rest of Cleveland.

With what my parents called the cynicism of the city, the Jacksons held our association with the Emmers in contempt. I suspected that Darwin's father had discussed my parents' connections to the Left with his son, but my friend (tactfully, I now feel) rarely mentioned the subject after I brought it up a few times. He could not, however, totally restrain himself. Once, as I was waiting for the bus, Jack Emmer passed by in his car, pulled to the curb, and shook hands with both of us. When he drove off, Darwin Jr. remarked disgustedly, "Those are the people you think are so smart."

I said nothing.

Darwin looked down at his elegant leather shoes and spat. "What?" asked Darwin a little angrily. "Makes you think that they know anything?" When I didn't respond, Darwin, with the earnest straightforward confidence of intelligent high school students everywhere, concluded forcefully, "They are white. They know nothing, and you know less."

CHAPTER SIX

Circle Pines: The First Time

During the summer of 1964, I spent a month at Circle Pines, a left-wing camp and resort not far from Kalamazoo, Michigan. The Emmers' children, Toby and Howie, went to the camp regularly, and Jack recommended it to my parents for me. I went at the beginning of July after emerging from my summer school class in algebra with the highest grade in the class. My pediatrician, Dr. Saunders, had growled—in his best Old World Jewish manner—that it was obvious that I had a brain, if I would just use it.

My stay at Circle Pines had been planned early during the spring semester in the midst of my academic collapse. I was going to SPU and reading a great deal, but drifting. Although Jack and Ruth conceived of SPU and the civil rights movement as political education for their children, an appropriate introduction to the Left's world of ideas and civic affairs, my stay at Circle Pines was intended more as therapy for a bright drifting youth than as political indoctrination.

The camp, run by a co-op in Chicago, still exists amid the Michigan woodlands outside Kalamazoo. Founded in the thirties, it was part of the co-op movement started to organize farmers around their political interests. The Circle Pines Cooperative had an active branch in Hyde Park and continued to do so while I was a graduate student at the University of Chicago in the early seventies. Many of the campers were leftists or the children of leftists. During the day, the young people engaged in work: gardening and the construction of cabins, latrines, and bathhouses for future campers. Late afternoons were spent practicing folk arts: learning to make ceramics and play guitar and baroque music on recorders and other wooden instruments. Older campers, often the youths' parents, conversed with each other at leisure. A few lower-class black youths from the inner city worked in the kitchen. They did not participate in the morning work program or the camp's social events. During the hot, sunny midwestern afternoons, however, campers and workers alike went to the shore of a huge lake where they sunbathed, swam, and canoed.

Arriving at the camp, I was assigned to a group of campers my age. Before dinner, a tall girl with long hair played a piece of music on the piano. That night—it must have been a Saturday—I attended a camp square dance in a barn brightly lit by Japanese paper lanterns. Along with square dances, Jewish folk dances, and Greek dances, there was a Danish pillow dance. Three or four girls wandered within a circle of campers and adults, each settling herself—at a significant pause in the music—before a boy and then embracing him. A short pink-cheeked girl, intrigued perhaps by a shy, dark newcomer, kneeled to face me and encircled my shoulders with her arms, holding me tight against her. I remember little else of the night. I did not go to sleep until four, and I awoke at three on Sunday afternoon, well after our family's hour of worship. The girl's kiss and my lengthy slumber seemed to separate me as completely from my family as the departure of their Ford station wagon the previous day.

At the Cleveland Institute of Music, I studied piano with Mrs. Apple, a short, frizzy-haired black woman who drilled me in scales. I got as far as the Chopin preludes and the Bach two- and three-part inventions. At a certain point I flagged as the relatively difficult compositions overcame my clumsy fingers and hopelessly faulty sense of rhythm. One particularly frustrating day, under the pretext of showing me how to interpret Chopin, Mrs. Apple explained to me the mode of romantic piano style, playing for me a series of excerpts from Beethoven, Chopin, and Liszt, discoursing all the while on the late eighteenth- and nineteenth-century culture of western Europe. I listened to the music rapt, amazed at the beauty of an art that seemed forever beyond me. At Circle Pines, sandal-clad girls deftly mastered the difficult fingerings and intricate rhythms that had defeated me. They performed with exuberance Mozart piano sonatas for four hands, improvised multiple-part harmonies on early Beatles tunes, and hummed snatches of Bessie Smith tunes at night to the chirping of the forest crickets. These young people flaunted an intimacy with books and authors I knew only by name. In the pockets of the older boys' leather jackets were Camus' *The Rebel,* Kierkegaard's *Either/Or,* and Richard Wright's *Native Son*—already an established literary classic among the young campers' parents, an earlier generation of Hyde Park radicals. After dinner I found in an airy lamp-lit room recordings of Paul Robeson, Marian Anderson, Benjamin Britten, and Kurt Weill on brittle seventy-eights. Sitting in the yellow light, I played these records again and again, sometimes, I can now admit, until they broke.

And for the first time in my life, a girl paid attention to me for more than a few days. She was a slender, brown-haired, bespectacled girl of medium height. I was taken by the unathletic way in which she walked, the black-and-red lumber jacket she wore early in the morning, and the distracted look on her face. On hikes, she bumped along beside me, prodding me into conversation.

Excited by an idea or piece of knowledge, I could be a garrulous talker. But how restrained a person I was when confronted by an interested girl! No girl I had ever thought much of had ever touched me on the arm in conversation and invited me, on her own initiative, to a secluded place. Looking at the campers around me at dances, on hikes, and on the beach, I discovered this casual eroticism everywhere. Even the folk dancing, with its sashaying approaches, face-to-face confrontations, and lingering withdrawals, seemed to provoke one to seek further erotic knowledge.

As I talked to the girls in my group, their casual profanity struck me in a similar way. The curses of these young people seemed to be less for the sake of obscenity than for emphasis. The expletives "shit," "fuck," "damn," and "hell" were usually used to express frustration with a shovel of mortar or disappointment with a brick and in no way resembled the elaborate obscene gestures of my older classmates at Alexander Hamilton. The profanity of my campmates represented not an act of defiance but the play of children at ease not only at home but throughout their neighborhoods. Listening to my camp friends' casual curses, I knew that I could never acquire anything but a shadow of their freedom.

The blacks at the camp were primarily seventeen- and eighteen-year-olds who worked in the kitchen. I saw them preparing food in the back of the dining hall during the early afternoon. After dinner, I saw them scrubbing the large brass pots outdoors and sweeping the dirt from the dining hall outside. I recognized their presence by the soul music that blared from the back of the kitchen. In particular, I remember two. One was a stocky dark girl who seemed to dress in a partially unbuttoned man's white dress shirt and blue jeans every day. The second was a tall, muscular boy of about eighteen. Also dark, he possessed sleek, substantial muscles revealed by snug white ribbed T-shirts. I remember him because he smoked in an aggressively masculine way, going through two or three cigarettes in a sitting, carelessly tossing his butts and used matches to the ground.

At some point that summer, I took a picture of a white girl who must have been sixteen or seventeen. In the background stands the black girl who worked in the kitchen looking at me from a distance. She looks ahead with one hand on her hip, her other arm hanging down by her side. Even from a distance I can make out her glare, both quizzical and stern. I did not think that she was very pretty and did not dance with her during the square dances. The boy, I remember, also gazed at me critically as he washed pots and peeled potatoes outside and I listened to my fellow campers strum their banjos and guitars or play baroque music in a consort of wooden bassoons and clarinets. He remained silent for a long time and after a few days finally spoke. He told me, with meaningful emphasis, that he listened to the Chicago radio station WVON because it played the music of black people. I recognized the subtle insult implicit in his words. A little shocked, I recovered quickly and told him that every white kid in my cabin had said that to me. I told him that I had become aware of the black struggle without the help of Smokey Robinson. In a sarcastic tone, he inquired, "I wonder?"

I did not like to spend long periods of time around the kitchen when either of the two kitchen workers was in sight. I came to understand their angry looks not from direct conversation with them but from what I overheard from my white campmates. As in Cleveland, middle-class whites in Chicago—even progressive left-wing Jews—had begun to leave their neighborhoods in the South Shore, Hyde Park, and Woodlawn for the western suburbs. They left behind a ghetto world that was in the process of acquiring a nationalist political consciousness amid the activities of gangs such as the Black Stone Rangers and the Disciples. The whites who remained took advanced classes at Hyde Park High or attended the competitive University of Chicago Law School, largely separate from blacks.

The anger of the black boy and girl, I surmised, reflected their bitter attitudes toward this racially divided world that promised racial integration as white liberals fled the ghetto for their own safety. A general sense of betrayal must have informed the alternately bemused, reproving, and angry stares of the two blacks. As in Cleveland, R&B and soul music in Chicago had become not just entertainment but a cultural symbol of opposition to the white world. Chicago blacks now lived in a world in which the gangs openly marched in the streets and recruited members in the black neighborhoods. The black boy and girl I observed in the kitchen were amazed that I had not yet gotten the word. Was I not in on what every black in Chicago already knew?

I could not escape my nagging guilt, only evade it. I threw myself into theater sometime midway into my stay at camp. When a play was proposed for the camp's second session, I eagerly joined the dramatic group. The first play considered was an English version of Jean Anouilh's *Antigone*, inspired by the work of Sophocles. The readings dragged on. And by the time a cast was assembled, everyone in the group had lost interest in the play. At some point, someone proposed with a casually grandiose gesture that we stage a production of Rodgers and Hammerstein's *Oklahoma*. This suggestion was taken up immediately—somewhat improbably, it seemed to me. The scale of the task daunted no one.

We read through the musical that afternoon and the following night. The play was cast with me as Ali Hakim, the traveling Armenian salesman. I had never acted in a play before. However, nothing could go wrong that summer, and my awkward, energetic appropriation of the part seemed in its own way right. I worked so hard that whatever anyone could have thought or said seemed irrelevant to me. I remember the lights at the foot of the stage, and the prompter who supplied the one or two phrases that I forgot. I remember the girls I kissed onstage. And I remember the tall brown-haired pianist from the dining hall, who seemed to me to have played all the songs perfectly during our first rehearsal.

The day after the performance, shortly before my parents came to pick me up, my emotions still soared like a kite in the April Cleveland winds. I had in my bumbling created a character that stole the show. As a joke I took the hand of a girl and kissed it. She immediately kissed me back. Somewhat dramatically, the tall willowy pianist approached me, her arms extended. Beginning with her hand, my lips climbed her arm with kisses. We ended in a long, deep embrace. I felt a million miles away from Lee-Harvard, and most exceptional.

Somewhere in western Michigan, I had donned a fedora to play an immigrant salesman in *Oklahoma* and heard sandal-clad girls improvising harmonies a cappella for early Beatles tunes and humming Muddy Waters blues to the accompaniment of guitars. These experiences had not been innocent. I had acquired a taste for slender white girls with long dark hair in peasant blouses, blue jeans, and dark-brown sandals revealing fresh white feet and nearly pink nails, a style that was made all the more erotic for me by its implicit rejection of the flashiness of the black teenage world around me in Lee-Harvard. It was not difficult to interpret the meaning of such tastes at the bus stop of Alexander Hamilton. In the world of Mount Pleasant, the girls I had kissed at Circle Pines were indistinguishable from other white girls per se. The burly German, Czech, and Polish children of immigrants in the Alexander Hamilton playground had warned people like me away from white girls. Everyone in Cleveland knew that approaching, much less kissing, white girls—whatever their political leanings—on Cleveland's East Side could be tantamount to risking my life.

Two weeks after leaving Circle Pines, I would go out West on a trip that I had won for accumulating a host of new subscriptions for my *Plain Dealer* paper route. Those two weeks in Cleveland, however, provided me with more than enough time to understand the gravity of my situation, to bring me back to earth. If I had lost touch with reality, I could expect to resume contact with terra firma in Lee-Harvard.

Daydreaming through my life—like daydreaming through any reality—had its costs, and I was soon to confront them on my trip out West. To tell the truth, I had been anticipating this explosion since that fall. Many of the young black paper carriers with whom I would travel to Colorado were tough city kids. I had seen them the previous winter at the *Plain Dealer*'s organizational meetings. The urban riots of 1964 would take place in Cleveland that summer, and much of the strange militant craziness of the black revolution had already been in the air the previous winter. At the meetings, the city kids sat defiantly in the pastel-colored plastic chairs in the *Plain Dealer*'s cafeteria. They cast insolent looks at the middle-aged ethnic white organizers. Their contempt was exacerbated by the full beards that they wore, then illegal in Cleveland schools. Many of them smoked elaborately carved brown-stemmed meerschaum pipes, inhaling the pipe's thick smoke into their lungs and blowing it out of their nostrils as if they were smoking cigarettes. Sitting together at the front of the room, they were already an entity of some sort—they seemed prepared to act, although it was not clear exactly what they were going to do.

On the bus to Colorado, I immediately chose an isolated seat away from the swaggering black mass from which a cloud of smoke and loud talk emanated. They had brought with them pint bottles of gin and rum along with playing cards. Absorbed in their own activity, they glanced at me only briefly before returning to their business. I felt free to enter a bookish dream world of the martial prelude to World War I and erotic dreaming. I vividly recall reading Barbara Tuchman's *The Guns of August* and a collection of Russian short stories entitled *New Soviet Science Fiction*. I was beginning to read well enough to be wholly absorbed in an elaborate literary world, and both books enveloped me in their historical or fictional realms. In the back of my mind was the summer's earlier adventure, and the subconscious residue of this experience bubbled up as I read. I remember in particular a passage in one of the science fiction stories in which a terrestrial space ship docks with an alien craft. Placing themselves in sight of the aliens, a man and woman strip and make love. Even as I now recall this scene, the image floats free of its encoded symbolism—the nature of human reproduction, the species' division of gender, and man's most important affectionate bonds—to illustrate desire itself. These, of course, were my desires. Wholly unsophisticated, I had little erotic release but this inward surge of excitement.

The sexual excitement was building among the rowdy black kids surrounding me on the train and the bus we took out West. On the train, they gambled and surreptitiously passed around their pints of liquor. Their emotions ebbed and flowed in surges of delight, anger, and sullenness. When we arrived out West, we transferred to large cross-country passenger buses with air conditioning and velvety thick-cushioned seats. At some point we found ourselves traveling alongside a busload of white girls about the age of our group.

Waving, blowing kisses, and pouting through the windows, they were as ignorant, disruptive, and ill kempt as our group. Apparently no more than two days from home, their hair was already dirty, and they were experimenting with lipstick and perfume purchased in the small towns where they had stopped. By coincidence, our groups lodged in the same hotel for two nights while we toured the local sites. The girls' rooms were quickly identified and their comings and goings closely watched by our group. Noisy flirtations, catcalls, and teasing ensued. One morning at the end of their stay, the girls joined hands and danced in a circle around our bus after we had all boarded. The ceremony was clearly a final provocation, retaliation for the surveillance they had endured for two nights. A deep emotional lull filled the bus after the girls' departure, a valley of feeling as intense as the earlier highs of sexual excitement. The boys squirmed restlessly, eager for action, angry at being stuck in the bus and having no physical outlet for their energy. We finally arrived at our last stop, a horse-riding camp in the snow-topped Colorado mountains. We would stay there in the thin mountain air for a week, three boys to a cabin.

I had managed to avoid notice by the rest of the group for a week, but amid their erotic restlessness, I became a natural target. Just what was I doing sitting alone and reading? Why did I seem to consider myself immune to their unhappiness? they seemed to be asking. In my cabin, I was finally noticed by two of the group's most violent members, boys I had gone out of my way to avoid. Sensing my fear with the quick intuition of the street, one of them set upon me. His attack as I wandered around absentmindedly was, I realized even then, inevitable. He was angry, much as my attacker in the Robert Fulton Elementary School playground had been years ago, for the simple reason that I just was not paying attention. My inattentiveness, I was now beginning to realize, signaled a sense of security to which no Cleveland Negro was privy. Who, he was asking, did I think I was? Did I not know that my dreaminess implicitly insulted him by removing him from my consideration? I knew enough of the streets to look behind me for the second boy who would be my true attacker, and as I turned to confront my inevitable second attacker, he set on me with angry fury. Punching my face and gut, he floored me in less than five seconds. It was, apparently, a spectacular display—as much for my collapse as for his skill. As he led me off to a cabin, one of our guides, a gnarled young cowboy, drawled with wonder, "You cannot fight, you cannot fight at all!"

I was put under the supervision of one of the cowboys throughout our stay in Colorado. Isolated from the general population, I was a particularly vulnerable prisoner. Darwin had a sharp tongue, and I knew that I could expect little sympathy from him upon my return to Cleveland. I already anticipated his dour look when I told him about my most recent collision with reality. The world was what it was, and black daydreaming paperboys among their peers high on Bacardi could expect to be beaten to the limits of their wits. I had been out of touch with reality for some time, I could imagine him thinking, and could expect just about anything to happen on my infrequent sojourns into the real world.

I went to visit the Jacksons shortly after returning home anyway. Whatever our differences, I was a fourteen-year-old black boy in Lee-Harvard, and I was as consumed by the gossip of the Alexander Hamilton playground as anyone else. I detected tension in the Jacksons' house as soon as I entered. In the same way that my parents harbored suspicions about Mr. Jackson's angry racial politics, the Jacksons disliked them for their headlong integrationism. As I recall, Darwin and I spent the afternoon racing small electric cars around the track that he sometimes set up on the ping-pong table in his basement. My refusal to talk with him about girls, parties, and dating—the ordinary interests of adolescent boys—revealed as much as it hid. At some point Mr. Jackson came down to the basement to tell me pointedly that Darwin had been growing up that summer. He had a job in the kitchen of a restaurant, had joined the local bowling league, and had a girlfriend. Mr. Jackson could not have expressed himself more clearly. Darwin was confronting and mastering the world before him—the world of sex. I had been ignoring the realities of black adolescent life while I was in western Michigan.

Somewhat rattled, I made a few remarks about camp to Darwin after his father returned upstairs. "We spent two weeks building a cabin," I reported. "We gathered stones, mixed concrete, set wooden forms, built walls up to the level of the roof."

"Let me get this straight," Darwin responded, now somewhat annoyed. "You paid to go to a camp where you built the house where you slept."

I ignored this.

"In the evenings," I said, "we sang, listened to music, or danced."

"What kind of dances?"

"Square dances, Greek dances, Jewish folk dances."

"After that," Darwin grimaced, "I guess you went out to the woods and fucked the Greek dancers."

I glared at him. He returned a pointed, tight-lipped stare. This lasted only briefly. He stepped back from the ping-pong table, composed himself, and placed his model car back on the electric track. It was a wholly adult gesture, a symbol of his mature exasperation with what to him was an utterly predictable account of my childishness.

I don't recall saying much more to Darwin about Circle Pines. He was part of the world that I had been so glad to escape. And he, for his part, was too occupied with navigating teenage life to care about how I spent my summer. Nor did I talk much to him about my intellectual interests. Returning to Cleveland, I immersed myself in classical music; however, my piano playing did not improve. I remember buying, with what little pocket money I had from my paper route, recordings of the Mozart symphonies, and listening to Symphony No. 41, "Jupiter," over and over again. I also listened to the Beethoven piano concertos, discovering Rudolph Serkin and acquiring as many of his records as I could. I listened to WCLV, Cleveland's classical music station, and began to learn about the composers, performers, and works the station played. And I persuaded my parents to let me use my paper route money to study classical guitar—which I learned to play about as poorly as I did the piano.

Returning to Cleveland in the late summer of 1964, I found that the city had entered a new period in its history. The anger of young black people in inner-city Cleveland now began to manifest itself as violence. Policemen were routinely called to answer calls for help from teachers confronting out-of-control students. Robbery, always a problem in the schools, reached a new high. My father was even more frequently called in to respond to suspected robberies at four or five in the morning. He was responsible for entering the buildings to open the schools' outside and interior doors while the police waited in their squad cars until he returned.

My father, now after ten years a full-fledged custodian and building supervisor, had full responsibility for maintaining the school buildings during this period of turmoil. During the year, he managed ever-more recalcitrant maintenance crews, which required an increasingly firm hand. As he attempted to fulfill his responsibilities, he began to encounter the ever-worsening indifference of black workers, their sense of alienation, and their contempt for the norms of workday life. Amid the ongoing social disintegration of ghetto life, his new cohort of workers lacked not only seriousness but also the most basic discipline.

My mother had begun to work as a teacher in Cleveland's Head Start. There she encountered the domestic side of the social disintegration that my father was seeing in the schools. She began to see homeless children and young boys and girls abused by their mother's boyfriends. She encountered young mothers wholly without the inner psychological means to run a household or nourish a family, and she also began to encounter the growing black radical presence in Hough and Glenville. Young black men, as everyone in the Community United Head Start program seemed to know, were gathering guns as if in anticipation of the forthcoming riots.

My parents were bewildered by this transformation and talked about it endlessly at the dinner table. Long an advocate of continuing education, my mother arranged with a local community college to place teacher-educators in an associate degree program for early childhood education. This was a highly successful project; many of her students graduated and became teachers and assistant teachers in Head Start, and the program became a pathway out of the depths of ghetto life. But she could be as fascinated by the failures in her program as by the successes. By the end of the first term, it was clear that some students were simply going through the motions of their academic programs. Their young white radical and liberal professors would then phone my mother, asking her permission to give these students grades lower than C. By the next semester, these students were maintaining D averages. They would inevitably eventually drop out of Cuyahoga Community College, Head Start, and public life itself. My mother would later see them stepping out of new Electra 225s in silk dresses on their way to marathon card games in ghetto apartments boasting huge new Sony color TVs. The emergence of this new leisure class was a continuing mystery to my mother, who had, after all, given up a graduate fellowship at Bank Street College to move to Cleveland, work full time, and raise a family.

Seen in retrospect, the riot that erupted in 1964 seemed the inevitable consequence of the racial tensions that had been building for some time. On Sundays in the late fifties, an elderly black woman named Mrs. Watson would visit my grandmother in our Mount Pleasant home on 137th Street. She and my grandmother would talk endlessly about religion. I couldn't follow much of what they said, but I do remember one of their discussions of the image of the moon turning into blood in Revelations. I was (and continue to be) caught by that image because it seemed to sum up the end of the world, which I could only imagine as a late-night terror show. The biblical apocalypse now seemed to me to be the coming of the ghetto to Lee-Harvard: the result of the overaged junior high school students smoking and drifting about the playground, the thugs in the high school ripping thermostats off the walls, and, more ominously, the militants in the streets. Even the music of the Temptations, the Miracles, and the Four Tops seemed, in their deep coital beat, to be moving toward a climactic moment that was as erotic as it was political. Later in puberty, I would recognize this anticipation of a new heavens and a new earth as a sexual urge as well as of a revolutionary political movement. The envisioned social transformation was as much an affair of erotic as political desire.

When I was in tenth grade, my parents declared that I must take financial responsibility for my college education. They could not afford tuition at a major private university such as Western Reserve. I would in all likelihood have to attend Cuyahoga Community College and receive excellent grades there if I were to have any hope of attending a first-rate liberal arts college. In ninth grade, I had put my nose to the grindstone, studying long hours every night and on the weekends, and in the tenth grade I had begun to receive all A's. I had escaped Cleveland once. I could do it again.

The music, dress, and swaggering on the street had evolved into something that appeared to be adversarial in more than a cultural way. One felt this in the amused contempt with which my schoolmates regarded the Beatles. I had heard an interesting discussion of this issue of racial authenticity a year before in a surreptitious study hall conversation. Looking at a publicity picture of the Beatles in gray suits with black fringed collars, two of my black classmates observed that young black boys in Glenville had been wearing such suits for years with absolutely no recognition from the press. Not only had the Beatles stolen and trivialized black music; these white boys from England had appropriated the cultural energy of a black society that had absolutely nothing else to sell. The Beatles had done this, moreover, to the applause of white critics who knew no better.

Predictably, my friend Darwin, unlike myself, grasped the politics of this cultural change. An excellent student in the ninth grade, he became an extraordinarily popular school leader. He was out and about in a way that I couldn't imagine being, with no visible negative effect on his classwork. Everything his father had said that summer upon my return from Colorado turned out to be true. On weekends he played basketball. He held a part-time job. And two or three nights a week he bowled with a club. He had a girlfriend—the light-skinned daughter of a police officer. He organized school dances, participated in the student council, and at the end of our tenth-grade year ran for class president.

His strategy was simple. Instead of only giving a speech, as was the custom, he made contact with the whole student body from top to bottom. He was shaking hands with and reaching out to not only the Major Work students but the hoods crowding around the school doors during class. Finally, he crafted a campaign speech that spoke to the mood of the students. Interspersed with his campaign promises—most of them concerning more dances and entertainment—were lines from the music of the Four Tops, the Supremes, and the Miracles. The students, already largely in favor of Darwin, yelled and howled in recognition of the lyrics. The auditorium seemed on the verge of riot. Most surprised was the student council faculty advisor, my French teacher Ms. Brady, who had reviewed the speeches ahead of time. She had apparently, according to Darwin, only circled the lyrics in red ink and placed question marks beside them. When I questioned Darwin about slipping the R&B lines past my favorite teacher, he told me pointedly that anyone could see that Ms. Brady had no idea who Eddie Dozier or the Temptations were.

In the ninth and tenth grades, I began to read with greater seriousness than I ever had before. I discovered books by major authors I could read with understanding. The first was Sinclair Lewis, whose treatment of white middle-class life meant much to me as I began to observe the world around me. Next I read John Dos Passos's *The Big Money,* a documentary novel whose language and literary technique held me in awe for weeks. I discovered the Sunday *New York Times* and the *New Yorker,* and I read their feature articles about art, education, the civil rights movement, and poverty over and over again. In these publications I discovered writers to whom I would return—Robert Coles, Erik Erikson, Kenneth Clark, Howell Raines, and Joseph Lelyveld—as well as many minor writers whom I read with great interest.

The differences between Darwin and me became more marked. At some point late in the spring, he received a bowling ball as a present from his father. The ball cost three hundred dollars, a price that still strikes me as remarkably exorbitant. Its custom-drilled holes may have accounted for its price. Darwin's fingers were exceptionally long, and the thumb hole, as I remember, was placed at a lengthy distance from the two finger holes. As I examined the ball in my hands, Darwin discussed the way in which the ball was weighted off center. The holes' position and the ball's displaced center of gravity made different kinds of spins useful in various situations possible, all of which Darwin went on to describe. I looked carefully at the ball. Why on earth, I thought, would someone bowl? What was the point of knocking down pins? Furthermore, what was the point of all these expensive technical refinements? I said nothing. And after a few minutes, Darwin, sensing my indifference, grew angry. He looked at me, stepped back a little, and smirked. "You think," he said incisively, "that you know more than anyone else."

I worked with all the momentum that Darwin, still an excellent student, was now investing in his social life. I had caught up to him academically; I was receiving straight A's and would surpass him in class rank that year. I pursued my new interest in school aggressively. Darwin and the class's other top student, Judy Patton, had by the second half of the year already told me that the pursuit of high grades for their own sake did not mean anything to them; however, this was no sign of academic slacking. (Both would become successful doctors and specialists, Darwin an ob-gyn and Judy a dermatologist.)

Late in the year, as I was riding home with Mr. Jackson one rainy afternoon, he began talking about Darwin's various activities. I realized quickly that he was giving me an indirect lecture. Seemingly out of nowhere he suddenly remarked, "You work too hard,"

I said nothing.

"You work too hard," he repeated. "What do you expect to get when you work so hard?"

"I want to go to a good college," I answered.

"After that?" he continued.

I said, "To a good graduate school."

"And after that?" he responded.

I said nothing. I was growing angry. He, after all, had met his wife in grad school. His remarks concerned not only my obsession with school but also my involvement in Circle Pines and SPU. He saw all this as wasted energy that might have been directed toward more practical matters. What did these activities have to do with my future and my aspirations? he was asking. Did I have aspirations? What could I reasonably expect my future to look like? It occurred to me that he was lecturing me because he assumed that I had not thought these things through, and I was offended. He seemed to be saying that because I was black, I was condemned to reconcile myself to the world's limited expectations for me. Was I living in another world? He was right, but moreover, I was beginning to develop a contempt for what I took to be the limitations of the black world.

CHAPTER SEVEN

Circle Pines Once More

My parents had been watching the developments in Lee-Harvard during this time. The riots occurring after ninth grade appeared to them to be the culmination of the anger, social disarray, and growing political militancy that had been emerging in the ghetto for some time. They had observed with contempt the rebellious posturing of lower-class black life. Sitting with Lucy Haug's mother during a student program in the Hamilton auditorium, my mother observed with despair and amazement not only the banal, poorly prepared program onstage but the unruly black male students in the aisles noisily proclaiming the nihilism that would become rap in the eighties. Driving me down Lee Road from a Student Peace Union meeting, she pursed her lips and clucked her tongue at a crowd of do-ragged blacks in a pale-pink late-model Cadillac convertible, a display of ghetto leisure and the conspicuous consumption of luxury goods purchased without regard for any rational economy.

As I became a better student, my mother's contempt for the inadequacies of John F. Kennedy, the newly built high school in Lee-Harvard, grew. The guidance counselors there recommended that I be placed in a private school, and my mother demanded that the Cleveland Board of Education pay the tuition. The board agreed to do this. After the riots, a number of New England prep schools had opened their doors to high-achieving young black students, and perhaps my grades won me the attention of one of these private school outreach programs. The possibility of my attending one such school was discussed by my parents and guidance counselors. However, I suspect that my withdrawal from the school's social life, my clear vulnerability to the lower-class thugs now filling the school, and my disoriented self-presentation, a product of the crazy jumble of ideas in my head, led the school's authorities to wish me gone. The increasingly volatile political situation created by the riots probably also played a role in their decision.

That summer I was selected to participate in a special program for tenth-grade students in the Cleveland area at Cleveland State. I took a course combining politics and literature taught by a fiery teacher from South High School, Mr. Koburna, and a chemistry course that foreshadowed my future collapse in the sciences. Mr. Koburna's class touched upon the subject of totalitarianism. We read Arthur Koestler's *Darkness at Noon,* and somehow I became aware of Koestler's collection of anti-communist essays. We may also have read George Orwell.

I remember little directly about Mr. Koburna's class. However, it confirmed some of the loose intuitions I had about the Left as I had encountered it in the Emmers, in SPU, and at Circle Pines. My parents subscribed indiscriminately to newsmagazines, and I had grown up reading anti-communist articles in *Reader's Digest* and *U.S. World Report.* I was struck because, on the strength of my admittedly superficial reading in magazines as well as books about World War II and postwar Europe, I had thought of Hungary, Poland, and Czechoslovakia as totalitarian states. As authoritarian regimes, these countries closely monitored the political views of their citizens and outlawed opposition political movements. I opposed socialism not so much as a political system as for its attack on individual freedom and, as far as I could tell, the individual.

At some point I went to see the movie *Closely Watched Trains.* I went out of naïveté, largely drawn by reviews of the movie that I had seen in the *Cleveland Plain Dealer* and probably ads boasting the praise of prestigious film critics. As I watched the movie, I realized that it was an attack on the East German authoritarian state. The movie ran against the grain of SPU's easy acceptance of the eastern European totalitarian states as a political reality that must be accepted as a kind of fait accompli. The movie, as I recall, put me in a kind of agony about the politics endorsed by SPU and the facility with which its members accepted certain political positions in the absence of literary or even historical reflection. All this struck me because, in my naive schoolboy way, I was beginning to regard my black classmates as not only anti-intellectual but also potentially authoritarian in their detached, cool postures and their repression of any passionate opinion. With my admittedly partial grasp of Koestler, Orwell, Arendt, and Koburna, it seemed to me that the Left with which I was acquainted had never undergone an adequate examination of the totalitarian and authoritarian impulses of the communist state it casually endorsed.

However, my awareness of the politics now emerging on the streets of Mount Pleasant and the world of Cleveland Heights had already begun to collide. Mrs. Haug, a tall, stately woman, represented an older European intellectual world of cultivation and the highest intellectual standards. Her radical politics was part and parcel of a bourgeois dignity. And this dignity, whatever her politics, was at odds with the freewheeling black culture on the streets. A variant of the same cultivation existed in the Emmers. I had come to realize by the summer of the tenth grade that these people had been, in some way, waiting for a revolution in American life, a Marxist class-based revolution that had never come. They were Communists of the old school—a distinction of which I had just become aware—and instead of wrestling with the problem of adjusting their progressive ideals to the realities of American democratic life, they had passed down their radicalism and their deep ambivalence about American life to their children. Circle Pines, I realized, was the site of an attenuated radicalism of earlier generation of leftists. These genteel political radicals had, in the early sixties, placed their hopes in a civil rights movement that was growing increasingly militant, as could be seen when some black members of the Cleveland branch of CORE began to refuse to sit with the white members. In Cleveland Student CORE, I participated in workshops concerned with the integration of housing in Cleveland Heights and Shaker Heights. However, I increasingly began to see that the white youths demonstrating against segregation in Cleveland's near eastern suburbs came from families that had moved to Cleveland and Shaker Heights in response to the expanding black ghetto that had so bothered Mrs. Haug and my mother in the auditorium of Alexander Hamilton. Ultimately, it seemed that even whites sympathetic to the black struggle must seclude themselves from the social breakdown of the inner city.

The real political action in the city, even with the biracial cooperation in the school integration movement, existed among blacks. The angry swaggering of black East Side teenagers had in the past few years become a political force. Darwin's use of R&B to reach the black student masses when he ran for student council had been in this vein. One saw the energy of Darwin's Alexander Hamilton audience among the city's Student CORE members, who one night gathered for a rally at Antioch Baptist Church. They sang civil rights songs, filling the church auditorium halls and sanctuary with far more emotion than I had ever heard in any hymn sung by the church choir. My white peers in the suburban unit of Student CORE were the nominal leaders of this rally, but its energy—the motor of its political force—clearly came from the blacks. Separatist impulses were becoming increasingly apparent in the movement, and by 1966 and 1967 these black teenagers were making it clear that the movement belonged to them.

In the summer of 1968, Carl Stokes's campaign for the mayoralty was underway. He had cultivated enormous support among blacks, who were on their way to becoming the city's ethnic majority. The riots of 1964, Cleveland CORE—whose black members had begun to separate from whites—Mayor Ralph Locher, and ex-judge and school superintendent Jim McAllister had failed to manage the city's serious emerging ethnic conflicts. This conflict was now coming to a head in a political crisis. Stokes ran not only with the support of the black community, whose allegiance he had won as an activist state senator working on their behalf, but also as the pragmatic choice of a business community that feared the financial consequences of Locher's incompetent management of the city's racial politics. Stokes spoke to a gathering of all the students in the Cleveland State program that summer. He wore an elegant summer suit and a striking silk tie. Although still a candidate, he already looked on top of the city's problems. He already looked like the winner.

My parents referred to Carl Stokes as Carl, remembering when he lived in Mount Pleasant and they'd pass him on the street as they went to Lawson for a gallon of milk and some ice cream. However, one could not disregard the fact that Stokes had emerged from the ghetto world of Central during the second wave of migration in the twenties. He had dropped out of high school to become a hustler on the streets and only reentered school after serving in the army. He had been on the police anti-liquor squad and largely built his political base among the city's churches whose spiritual fervor was too freewheeling for my parents—the "primitive" Baptist, Pentecostal, and AME black churches—and what my mother called "the city," that is, the world of sharpies, numbers runners, and the mob. One could also not disregard the fact that the young Stokes had gotten his professional start primarily as a "lawyer" in the city, handling criminal cases in the common pleas court, minor real estate cases, and divorces. His political base was everything my parents had fled since moving from Glenville. However, one could not doubt that he and the black urban culture he represented had become the city's most potent political force.

The new black radicalism had reached Circle Pines by the time that I arrived for my second stay. I rode to Circle Pines with the Ormond family. Mr. Ormond was an oboist in the Cleveland Symphony Orchestra, and Mrs.

Ormond, Mimi, was a teacher at Park Synagogue and one of the radicals who had arranged for my mother to be hired at Park Synagogue. They questioned me about my education in the way that any bright fourteen-year-old might expect to be questioned in such a context. When I replied that the next year I would attend University School, a local private school that had given me a scholarship, there was a nearly universal murmur of approval, the lone dissenter being Sol Levin, an elderly Jewish leftist tailor and the father of a classmate, Becky, who had been involved in radical politics. His style of Marxist theory and practice, probably acquired in the thirties, was as stern and unyielding as my mother's belief in high bourgeois culture. He quietly but firmly stated that I should rise with the masses rather than against them. There in the car I heard the hard, direct tone of the labor union organizer going about his task. One found hints of this position elsewhere. There was disgust in some quarters over the fact that I spent more time listening to people playing Bach and Corelli on the bass recorder than to ragged renditions of Muddy Waters. As a Negro, I had responsibilities to my people—and suddenly these responsibilities seemed to include certain cultural tastes as well.

I received my most severe comeuppance for my aberrant behavior from black members of a civil rights group from Greenwood, Mississippi. This group arrived one sunny afternoon in a bus, immediately went to an elevated area outside the dining hall, and shouted, "Freedom now!" the signature cry of CORE.

At night some of the black southern civil rights guys slept in our cabin. For some reason, I had naively conceived of the young civil rights workers in the South as angelic youths threatened with violence by older bigots. But I was quickly disabused of this belief. Upon learning I was from Cleveland, one of the older civil rights workers—he was probably sixteen or seventeen—quickly, and with impressive geographical accuracy, launched an attack upon "those uppity niggers living in the 140s and 150s and in Lee-Harvard, thinking they got something and got nothing." He and his friends shared a lascivious account of their conquests among the white female civil rights workers, who had allegedly come to them, inviting their own sexual conquest by these black teenagers. The civil rights workers spoke in heavy southern accents and were contemptuous of anyone who contradicted them. This was strong stuff bordering upon sexual and racial insult, but it also was typical male boasting.

These guys had no use for me, and I quickly tired of them. One night, trying to get to sleep, I challenged the noisiest one.

"What do you do when you get these girls pregnant?" I asked. "Doesn't Mississippi have enough stray brown babies?"

"Shut your mouth, you silly goose," he replied. "Your tongue wags like a broken fence."

"You silly black baby," said the other. "What you going to do when a white girl opens your pants and pulls out your dick? Will you keep talking then?"

"Shut the fuck up!" howled one of the white guys from across the cabin.

"You could make me, motherfucker, if you weren't afraid of your own dick!" was the final reply.

This response left a dead and empty silence lingering through the room like gray afternoon thunderclouds over the green Michigan cornfields outside Kalamazoo. Five minutes later the white boys took up the conversation again as if nothing had happened.

I had little sense of irony at the time, but I did remark that the southern blacks clearly saw these liberal and leftist whites as incredibly naive. Whether true or false (I realized even then that oral histories of the civil rights movement would be just as loaded with braggadocio as the legends of any other movement), the blacks' tales were intended to shock and intimidate the whites. The Mississippians had discovered a very real soft spot in the psychology of these suburban leftists: the fact that many of them were moving out of Chicago's South Side to the suburbs. I suspect that these civil rights workers, who must have well known what guilt and fear smelled like, quickly sniffed them out among their white counterparts and exploited it as insecure people will in unfamiliar circumstances.

And, of course, much of this object lesson in white impotence and black power was largely meant for me. Clearly I hadn't learned my lesson from the streets, from the blacks at camp, or from my parents—who did I think I was, hanging around tired communists, sopping up a dead white culture, flirting with girls who wanted something quite different, and playing Marian Anderson's overly refined versions of the spirituals? Whoever I thought I was (and this was a matter of considerable conjecture), I was in fact totally mistaken about my identity. Everybody knew what it was to be black.

Whatever such a person as myself thought, the world's impression of him was clear: he could only be a fool in the eyes of other blacks, and a buffoon to the whites, who might tolerate him out of cynicism or an incredibly childlike ignorance of the world. This, I thought, was their judgment, and it carried a truth that I felt even if I did not understand it.

I was deeply afraid that a couple of them would corner me and beat me up. They noticed this, and one of them called out to me one day, "Don't be afraid, goosie. De Lawd"—their mocking name for Martin Luther King—"says we is nonviolent."

This remark did not allay my terror when late one night I stumbled upon one of the black civil rights activists lolling with a girl as I walked back to my cabin through the woods from a square dance. Startled, the boy lifted his head. The girl lurched, her freckled breasts revealed by her opened blouse. Recognizing me, the Mississippian relaxed and smiled, gently calming his girlfriend as she pulled her blanket around herself.

"Little goose," he said, looking up at me. "Don't you know not to go where you don't belong?"

CHAPTER EIGHT

University School

When I entered University School on scholarship in the fall of 1966, I realized that the gray, empty world of urban Cleveland was the husk left behind by a WASP elite departing for such places as the sloping fields of Claythorne and Brantley. As I walked along the school's circular drive that fall, I saw signs of Cleveland's suburban wealth and power. The son of the editor of the *Cleveland Plain Dealer* was driven to school every morning in his father's Jaguar, the sleek red European sedan elegantly moving among the wood-trimmed Ford station wagons of the Shaker Heights matrons. That fall, they all had the salmon-tannish glow that wealth seems to confer upon women of their class. My classmates dated the girls from US's sister school, Hathaway Brown, who walked past the campus in their school uniforms. It was, I soon realized, not a coincidence that many of these people shared the same last and middle names. These schools were where they reproduced not only families but wide-spread networks of kin. The most ambitious students at Kennedy and Hamilton carried briefcases and rushed through the crowded halls to class. The halls at US were, by my standards, only sparsely filled even between classes. There was no need to rush; these students had already arrived.

The foundation of this world was the wealth made in the factories and forges in which blacks, Slavs, Poles, Hungarians, Serbs, and Irish had labored in the forties, fifties, and sixties. My father had taught me about the human cost of these places. He had seen men electrocuted in the factories. Drowsy from lack of sleep, they touched the electrolytic vats, stiffened, and died. But everyone respected this power, including my father and the white magnates in Shaker Heights. When I was a young boy, he took me to West and East Side sites where workers had lost their lives and limbs. These old gray factories in Brook Park and elsewhere were, for him, somehow holy. For all their terrors, he showed them reverence.

At University School I needed some time to identify the understated gestures in which power expresses itself. These expression of power appeared where I least expected them: in the slight strut, the elegant postures, the unhurried stride of the wealthiest US students as they made their way from class to class. The self-conscious grace with which the headmaster served the ball with the American twist during a doubles match on Alumni Day, the way in which a senior might loaf on the couch in the library with a single book by his side, the erectness with which we stood when an adult entered the room—these were not empty gestures but expressions of wealth and power borrowed from New England prep schools.

The male WASP students, I noticed, loved to preen in a way that curiously brought to mind my pimping lower-class black classmates at Alexander Hamilton and John F. Kennedy. Preparing to sit down on the library couch, they would stand up ramrod straight, take great care to arrange their jackets and ties, and make a show of crossing their legs as they sat down. It took me some time to realize that these elaborate upper-class male displays were similar to the pimp refinements of the young men with do-rags on 135th and Kinsmen. It occurred to me that although I had never thought hard about what manhood was, I was seeing it now—preening adolescent white manhood—in these delicate boys from Shaker Heights. Among their black brethren in the inner city, this preening was a mimicry of power. Here in Shaker Heights among pink-skinned males so delicate that they might be raped in the Alexander Hamilton boys' locker room was the reality of power. I gradually discovered that these gestures represented something more real—social status and wealth devolved to the wealthy's rising male children, who were now feeling their oats. I gradually realized that the affectations that I had been taught to reject all my life were aspirations to power reserved for the rich and their Yale- and Princeton-bound children who lived in mansions in Shaker Heights.

I best understood my place in this world by looking at the maids with whom I sometimes rode the bus up Warrensville to US. They would get off with me to walk in their employers' cast-off summer dresses to the imposing dwellings on Claythorne and Brantley. After we moved to Cleveland Heights, my mother would talk of meeting black maids who had gone to Glenville High School in the thirties and now worked for their white classmates. Although these black women might have run the vast households in which they worked, they were, as people, ultimately invisible to their white employers. My classmates, I suspect, accepted me in the same absentminded, patronizing way in which they accepted the black maids who had raised them from childhood. Their families had long cultivated congenial ways of imposing racial order in their households. Not only was I invisible, but they would, quite without realizing what they were doing, retaliate when I forced them to notice me for myself.

I soon felt that my becoming part of the school and its traditions would be an act of rebellion against the school's deepest sense of itself as a nesting place for Cleveland's elite, a midwestern version of the New England prep school enclave. The strongest form of resistance I could exercise was projecting myself into the very life of the institution. The pervasive, if understated, expressions of power offered a way in which this might be done. Like everyone entering the school through its main entrance, I passed a wall of pictures that was nearly thirty yards long. Many of the pictures were group pictures of the prefects and senior members of the honor society. The students were all dressed in maroon coats, white pants, and striped red-and-black ties. There were also pictures of small groups of preened seniors. Students, teachers, administrators, elegantly dressed businessmen alumni who had drifted in for lunch, and sometimes the cleaning people would stop to look at the pictures. They stared at the photos in the same way that Robert Frost wrote that people stare at the sea, gazing with casualness and passion, happiness and grief. People sometimes looked quickly at a particular class; sometimes they searched slowly to find relatives, friends, or people whose names they'd heard mentioned in passing. I doubt, however, that anyone spent as much time before these pictures as I did. I looked hard at the pictures—continuously, relentlessly, and indiscriminately—because there was nothing that I wanted more than to break up those lines of white faces. I spent a great deal of time considering—as I suspect many of my Jewish prep school friends did—how I would pose if and when my time came.

Those pictures symbolized the school's central task: the initiation of its young white charges into a world of wealth and power. And gradually the school's symbolic world imposed itself upon me not as a regime but as an organic cycle akin to the lives of the sycamores and maples along Claythorne: the blue oxford shirts, rep ties, expensive chino pants, brown penny loafers, woolen socks, and madras coats of early fall would by November give way to tweeds, gray woolen blazers, and pinpoint cotton shirts. As I followed the donning and shedding of these skins, these refined measures in which the school's heart lay—the richness of the wool in the tweeds, the width of the ties, and the length of shirt collars—made it clear that I would always be an outsider at this school. I had worn khakis and blue shirts all my life, but suddenly I was aware of the thinness of the material from which my pants were made, the shortness of the collars, the narrowness of the ties, and the vulgarity of my brown Hush Puppy buck shoes. Frustrated, I spent a day searching for the proper clothes. Only one department store at which my parents shopped had the kind of madras coat I wanted—and, to my surprise, it cost over two hundred dollars. I tried to imagine the kind of a person who would pay so much for a coat and found that I could not. All the same I was drawn to the school's heart of upper-class power and its reflection in the luxury around me. People sweating at the West Side forges had created the wealth that had purchased the library's rich brown leather couches and the vast playing fields. At its best, the lavish surroundings of the school made learning magical. I remember little of my first year other than reading Chaucer. By then I had studied French for about six years, and I was amazed at the way in which Middle English had absorbed French. I read and reread my Chaucer with both the thrill of discovery and the shock of recognition. I also remember a stunning course in American history, my first exposure to anything like the serious study of culture. I had not known that listening to Henry Adams on the Gilded Age or to William Bradford on the Plymouth plantation was to hear the re-creation of a world. I heard Glenn Gould's recording of *The Goldberg Variations* with the same sense of discovery.

By virtue of my interests and my odd, scattered reading, I found myself engaged in illuminating discussions with serious teachers. A history teacher whom I admired would take me aside and reflect upon the current literary dispute over William Styron's fictional account of Nat Turner. Another might discuss his previous lecture on A. E. Housman's *A Shropshire Lad* in class. Or the canny librarian and I might argue over Steven Kelman's *New York Times Magazine* article describing his observations and experiences as a first-year student at Harvard in 1967 and 1968. As a first-year student at US, I was amazed by the gravity of many of these discussions, and their lack of condescension. And curiously, given my experience at Circle Pines, none of this had anything that I could tell to do with race. Conversations in the hall or at the library desk, as far as I could make out, were offered not with ideological fervor, but with casual assurance that was lacking at Circle Pines and that had disappeared from Yale by the late sixties. The idea that an adult would take a student aside and talk seriously to him had, until now, been utterly beyond me.

During my first year at US, my tennis teacher, Peter Ebbot, and I got into an argument over social class. He gently and courteously explained to me while we were sitting by the court that his trust fund came from stocks in the coal industry, and that in the course of this company's operations several people were killed each year. He said that these people's deaths were an unfortunate but bearable inconvenience to him. We got into a heated discussion over this, but I was deeply grateful to him for telling me what he thought. This was forever happening. Once my history teacher, Dick McCrea, quoted to me Clarence Darrow's proposition that the wealth of the rich requires protection more than anything else in society. An arrogant but naive black kid who had assumed a facile radicalism, I found myself forced by the conventions of genteel conversation to think carefully. I was staggered in the way that everyone who for the first time encounters a truly oppositional point of view without adequate intellectual defense is staggered. I realized that I was encountering an honest statement in which someone had a real stake, as real a stake as the older leftists at Circle Pines. This stake was, moreover, taken for granted as a day-to-day reality visible in the factual existence of the sprawling stone and brick buildings around them.

In a way it was an act of defiance for the Jewish students to attempt to become part of this social order. And to watch their response to the task of becoming one with US was to learn a great deal. It was in the spirit of the school's cultivation that the community's brilliant Jewish students presented the greatest threat to the school's genteel WASP ethos. These students were the school's most troubling and disruptive presence. Jews had gone to US for some time but were now entering in increasing numbers. My classmates Richard Schwartz and Les Wolf were fully at ease with the means by which they were still kept from the heart of Cleveland's WASP elite. Yet they could respond to the school's anti-Semitism with their own scornful variations of our classmates' behaviors. Les, a gentle guy and the valedictorian of our class, would mock the WASP strut as he walked down the hall. In his locker, Richard kept not only two copies of the latest J. Press catalogs but also a small ruler with which he measured ties to ensure they broadened near the bottom to the currently fashionable width. He did this with a twinkle in his eye even as he commented on the acceptability of the colors and stripes of his classmates' ties. The Jewish elite could provoke incredible hostility among people who claimed to be their friends, although duplicity in friendship was expected at US. After one particularly striking string of Jewish winners at the annual awards assembly, Richard whispered to me, "Did you hear the sigh of relief after Scott Rogers took a prize?"

For me, the only road to school participation appeared to be academic. I found myself working harder with poorer results than ever before. During my first year at University School, I was devastated by the academic competition. I had been first in my class at John F. Kennedy, but during my first year at US my grades fell precipitously. School seemed to last all day, and there was gym—field, as we called it—in the late afternoon. After coming home, I slept for an hour or two then got up and did my homework and went to bed. I felt fortunate to be so tired since my fatigue made me forget the utter isolation that I felt.

It was impossible to keep my interests and new discoveries entirely from Darwin. I don't remember precisely what we talked about, but I do remember mentioning a book we were reading in class.

"Shut up," he said. "You're showing off."

I probably was showing off. More than anything, I wanted recognition from my classmates, from my friends, and ultimately from girls like the ones I had known at Circle Pines. I began to telephone Lucy Haug, the classmate who had invited me to SPU. We saw movies together, among them *Elvira Madigan,* which I remember as a blur of brilliant colors. Although she was very smart and her parents were intellectuals, she did not want to talk about books. She, I think, just enjoyed going to movies. These dates were a sobering experience. My parents agonized over whether or not we should be allowed to take the bus together before finally deciding that my father would drive us to the movies and pick us up afterword, while I agonized over what movies we would see and what we would do.

I began to realize what Mr. Jackson meant when he told me the previous summer that Darwin was growing up. Darwin's father meant that he was beginning to learn to communicate with blacks outside his immediate circle of male friends; he was beginning to discover what men and women did together in black Lee-Harvard. To use Darwin's words, I knew nothing—of this world. My classmate Lucy clearly knew what girls and boys did together in Cleveland Heights and at the left-wing camp she attended in Vermont. They went to the Newport Folk Festival, they went to coffeehouses in Greenwich Village, and they went to parties where there was European and Jewish folk dancing. All this dawned upon me and impressed itself upon my consciousness as we began to go out.

At one point during Christmas vacation she invited me to her home. Her mother, who was baking fruitcake, greeted me graciously. Once imprisoned, she was now in the midst of an incredibly successful academic career. Lucy came downstairs and invited me to her bedroom. Putting on a recording of *Aida,* she chatted beside me and then picked up her guitar. Soberly sweet, dressed in a miniskirt and leotard, she smiled during an awkward silence and handed me a book of Eliot's poetry opened to *The Love Song of J. Alfred Prufrock*. I gazed at her, taking her in. Looking at her—a vision of what I had wanted since leaving Circle Pines—I found myself dazed and paralyzed.

Shame is, as Marx wrote, a revolutionary sentiment. And in my embarrassment, I could only remember my father's question about the white girl in leotards at the Cleveland settlement house. The little white girl I was going to marry. Was I, he had asked me near the end of junior high, still going to marry her? I now knew the answer: she had nothing to do with my world. And neither did Lucy. I had not gone to left-wing camps in Vermont, read Eliot with enough understanding to know that I was a Prufrock in my bumbling courtship, or my mother's PhD dissertation in an authentically informed way. I did not play the guitar well or understand classical music, nor could I make sense of a world in which people did those things. The basic elements of Lucy's environment were not mine. I couldn't approach her because I did not know who she was or how her mind worked. This realization made me halt my advances as the light-brown hair of Prufrock's love object. Darwin, the Jacksons, and my parents disagreed furiously about the meaning of everything black in Cleveland, but they were comprehensible to me in a way that Lucy never was.

We chatted for another forty-five minutes before she—pleading that she had to get back to her homework—led me back downstairs. More out of discomfort than anything else, I looked helplessly at her mother, who was pouring rum over fruitcakes. She glanced at me and smiled. Lucy, now miffed, led me to the door, which she firmly closed behind me. We did not go out again. I understood perfectly why but continued to call her out of loneliness and out of habit. When I made my last call to her house, her father answered the phone, chuckling. "Three strikes," he said, "and you're out."

The next year, my grades improved dramatically. I turned my attention to my studies and found myself succeeding. By the end of the first trimester, I was fifth in my class. Doing well, I discovered, meant that you could, with perfect propriety, sneer at those who did worse. I found that this suited me perfectly, and I studied all the time, to the dismay of my father. I took world history with Mr. Sanders—a great teacher nicknamed "El Dios"—and got up at five on the morning of an examination to finish studying. My father inquired about this behavior to our pediatrician, Dr. Saunders, who had sent two of his sons to US. The doctor assured him that it was not only normal but good for me. I did not have much of a relationship with most of my classmates, but I felt great.

The importance of academic achievement to admission to elite colleges was undermining the sense of entitlement among students at US. The idea that a person is a bundle of talents, accomplishments, and achievement test scores was a new way of looking at human beings for me. I suspect it was also new to the most traditional elements at US, who had probably previously gained admission to good schools by virtue of their family accomplishments, wealth, and lineage. They were now threatened by the most intelligent students in their ranks, people who were often not the most ethnically acceptable to them and their families. Among members of the top quarter of the class, people were valued and dismissed on the basis of how well they did academically. Even in a provincial Cleveland prep school, one sensed that something about Cleveland's social structure was changing.

It was now not only blacks and Jews who in some sense threatened the school's sense of identity; Wealthy WASPs seemed to be afraid of the democratization of American society itself. For a long time, even the brightest seniors had limped along with C's and B's. In the new era of academic competitiveness, however, grades were all important. Over a decade before, University School had sent between a quarter and a third of its students to Harvard, Yale, and Princeton. It was now well known that Yale was admitting far more students from public schools than from prep schools; the new competitive class of public school test-takers with 1500 boards was now entering the elite universities in large numbers, and as admissions counselors were increasingly telling disgruntled parents, admission to Yale or Princeton was no longer the entitlement of four years of tuition at US. One sensed that at Columbia, Harvard, and Chicago, a new class was more than a little giddy about its arrival at the nation's traditional centers of power.

This change might have been most evident in my class's change of attitude toward Mr. Sanders's world history class. Most students took World History I and II during their senior year. The course consisted of a traditional narrative history of Western civilization from the Renaissance to the postwar period. At the heart of the class was a great deal of European political, military, and social history, all of which was to be memorized. Mr. Sanders's tests demanded a synthesis of information into coherent essays. The demands he made on his class were justified by his excellence as a lecturer and questioner. You had to be in his class to know that his sobriquet was not wholly a joke.

Earlier students at US had been willing to let world history slide. These boys were the sons of wealthy businessmen, and as future corporation presidents and managers, they were thinking more of the practical advantages of math and science. To do well in all their courses, they would have had to extend themselves during senior year, a time filled with private parties and proms. Nothing was worth giving up the ease and grace with which they approached the future. In my class, however, competition for grades was much more fierce all around, and I had never walked gracefully into anything. I still moved a little too fast in the halls, and I studied world history day and night, as intimidated by the tests as I was fascinated by what Sanders had to say in class. My class's high test scores in the course were a scandal, and Mr. Rickard, my eleventh-grade English teacher, joked at one point that Mr. Sanders was crushed.

I was completely overwhelmed by the world history tests and Mr. Sanders. One day I had my mother call me in sick in order to avoid a world history examination. I had done this only once before, to my parents' great displeasure. Tension was high at home after I skipped a second examination. The day after, my father went into work a little late so that he could drop me off at school. Much of life, he said, involves showing up in places one dislikes and being questioned about what one doesn't know. News of my absence on the day of the test quickly spread; my classmates were outraged, and an editorial was written attacking cheating (clearly a reference to what was seen as an attempt on my part to get an unfair advantage over my peers). Mr. Rickard remarked dryly that I had stimulated the literary efforts of some of the class's weakest students. I was not only embarrassed but a little scared. The school had been known to throw students out, and as cynical as I was, I was not sure that I had not misjudged the seriousness of what I had done.

A new Dean of Students, a tall bespectacled man, took me aside and, in a direct patrician manner, asked me a question that went right to the heart of the matter. Bearing down seriously upon me with his blue eyes, he asked me whether I wanted to be treated like everybody else. Did I want to be a part of this community? I was stunned and could not speak. Everything that he implied turned upon my tenuous membership in the school's community. Did I want my blackness to devalue my academic real estate—the only real property I had? He was an ex-administrator from the Cleveland Board of Education. He had helped design John F. Kennedy High School, that tall, windowless monstrosity whose administrators had told my mother to send me to prep school. He was a white man from Cleveland. And I—how could I have forgotten?—was a Negro from Invermere, my father was a janitor, and my mother was a colored schoolteacher. Did I know where I was? That summer a friend from Kennedy had called me up to tell me that Mr. Yuhass, our principal at Alexander Hamilton, had been cornered in the John Adams High School parking lot. He had been chased by a car carrying two or three black boys. This kind of thing did not go on at US. Crazy black kids did not dominate the school. The dean was laying it on the line for me. I could not speak. Someone, some white man, had seen through my greatest aspiration.

⟨⟩

The eleventh grade at US meant preparation for college. In the tenth grade at John F. Kennedy, I had been recruited for Columbia by a black graduate of the university. He was a newspaper editor, and he displayed—although I did not recognize it as such then—much of the Ivy League cockiness that I associated with US. He kept in touch while I was at US, and I simply assumed that I would go to Columbia or the University of Chicago, the two most urban and bohemian schools I could imagine. Except for one or two of my Jewish classmates, no one who cared enough to discuss the matter with me could make any sense of this. One of my classmates asked me why I didn't consider the University of Detroit instead of Chicago. He was a loutish, red-faced boy from the West Side, and I probably should have understood his question as a reflection of his ignorance of Chicago's prestige and as a racist reference to Motown.

As a black with an SAT verbal score of 700 and 700s on some of my achievement tests, I would be forgiven some of my less impressive scores. I could, it soon became clear, go anywhere, and I decided quickly that the social gauntlet I had walked at US entitled me to just this sort of privilege. I had gone on no more than two or three dates while at US, and it now occurred to me that what I wanted to do at college was chase girls and live the bohemian life that I had envisioned during the magical month of my first stay at Circle Pines. That summer, my father had taken me to Columbia for an interview. I was surprised at how grimy it was. The final grades were still posted by the office, and I was amazed at how many F's the teachers gave. I was not much moved; after all, it seemed that I had done nothing but study for the last few years surrounded by the kind of arrogant prep school types on the Columbia campus. But Columbia's harsh university air, filled by the sounds and smells of city, felt liberating. There were girls in leotards and short skirts, and I felt as if I was being invited into a new bohemian world.

My academic success won me acceptance elsewhere as well. The alumni clubs of Yale and Princeton were assisting their universities in the process of integrating their student bodies, and many of the leaders of these clubs had gone to US. I was invited to the law offices and homes of very well-to-do young men who were already vice presidents of corporations. I was flattered by this attention, which no one else I knew was receiving, and stunned by how wealthy, elegant, and still a little boyish, in the US mode, these men were. It was amazing to me that men just in their thirties should already be partners in law firms and officers of corporations. But even more amazing was the apparent decision that now blacks were to be a part of all this.

The summer after my junior year, there had been riots in Cleveland. At Circle Pines, I had tended to dismiss leftist theories of revolution, but this revolution in the streets and the schools was the logical extension of everything I knew about black Cleveland. Blacks had discovered power, and I was the beneficiary. Carl Stokes owed his election to the white business community's perception that the previous mayor, Ralph Locher, could not manage the city's increasingly militant black population. Nothing could have had a more concrete reality—not even the stone and bricks of US. Ironically, much of the militants' firepower had come from the city's frightened businessmen's foundation. Armed with automatic weapons that they had bought with Cleveland Now funds, the nationalists set buildings afire and waited for the firemen and police to arrive. The police, carrying only .38 caliber guns, quickly found themselves outgunned by the nationalists with high-power rifles. In this desperate situation, Stokes had wit enough to persuade streetwise young men to go into the streets and calm their fellows. The National Guard, armed with machine guns and protected by armor, was called. And shortly afterward, in a gesture aimed at keeping the peace in the ghetto, Stokes marched through the streets with the black nationalists. Condemned by the white policemen for having given in to the rioters, Stokes nevertheless staved off a far more serious urban disruption than the ones in Detroit and the black New York City ghetto and proved adept at negotiating a peace with the militants.

Deep down, everyone knew that University School was about nothing other than the power that had created wealth and then moved it from the city to Claythorne and Brantley. Clearly the social elite both in Cleveland and throughout the nation had begun to sense the potential danger of black power. Schools such as Yale and Princeton, and more specifically the powerful men who came out of them, were looking at my own motion from Mount Pleasant to Shaker Heights as an exercise of power, or at least something that looked, tasted, and felt like power. As such, I could be of global importance to them. One was increasingly hearing from the noisy advocates of black power that African Americans were a central part of a worldwide black revolution of the Third World nations against their colonies. Here was even more persuasive proof of what the significance of blackness might be.

I was buoyed by the approval of these Cleveland Ivy league alumni, many of them US grads, yet I was naive about the meaning that these revolutions had to them. I still planned to go to Columbia; however, I began to question these plans during the events of March of 1968, when apocalypse seemed to be in the air during the Columbia strike. That summer I was stunned not so much by the strike itself as by its anti-intellectual nature. I remember explaining this to my French teacher. The occupation of classrooms and the savaging of administrative offices was to me an attack on everything that the university represented for people who were primarily interested in reflection. I found this attack on civility horrifying.

I remember a *Newsweek* article that showed David Shapiro, a Columbia senior, reclining in President Grayson Kirk's desk chair in his office and smoking his cigars. Shapiro was already a recognized poet who would go on to achieve more fame. I looked at him hard and saw not only the future but the past. It was sometimes possible for me to think that the revolution in the streets of Hough and Morningside Heights had something to do with me. However, Shapiro's picture on the cover of *Newsweek* was both revelatory and prophetic. Bankrupt of any real political ideology of discipline, the Ivy League—with its new "meritocratic" constituency—had appropriated the "revolution" as a form of generational rebellion. One look at Shapiro's privileged face must have disabused me of this notion. I did not customarily associate the increasingly facile politics of the leftist kids I had known at Circle Pines with the haughtiness of my classmates at US. However, the children of Circle Pines' older, more sober leftists had already begun to experiment with the talk of the revolution during my last stay. For all their criticism of the alienating university, their primary concern was their own willfulness and gratification. It seemed to me that the upper middle class had appropriated the prideful anger of the New Left much in the same way they tried to appropriate the soul of black culture. The revolution in the universities was the revolt of the privileged against their fathers. The causes were not altogether clear. Surely the war in Vietnam had something to do with it, but even this rationale was too pat to describe this cohort's narcissism as politics.

My pediatrician, Dr. Saunders, had for the last fifteen years watched his young clientele participate in the academic sweepstakes that overtook Cleveland Heights, Shaker Heights, and the private schools every year. I knew of at least two of my classmates, Gary Shapiro and Les Wolf, who had been his patients since infancy. Les was going to Amherst, Gary was going to Princeton, and I might be going to Columbia. Dr. Saunders was proud but sober when I went for my checkup that year. He told my father that he had watched a young child in his care die of leukemia recently. It had shaken him up, and he wanted to talk about it afterward. He had, a short time before, told my mother of the many doctors and professors he knew with disabled children, children who could never live up to the academic and professional goals that their parents had set for their families. I suspect that he sensed the academic giddiness in the air that spring. Speaking of my friends' accomplishments, he started referring to the elite American schools as "those places." Dr. Saunders was a Canadian who had gone to McGill, and his children had been victorious in the academic competition. His daughter had gone to Smith, and his sons to elite schools. He honored academic accomplishment, but he knew that life was more than an IQ test. "Beware," he told me before I got into Yale. "Do not take the Ivy League's records of success too seriously. They are hospitals for healthy people." My classmate Richard Schwartz got an even more severe comeuppance. Upon his acceptance to Yale, he went to his rabbi in joy, boasting about his SAT score and his triumphs before the Ivy League admissions committees. The rabbi looked at him sternly and asked, "What makes you think that just because the numbers get higher, things get better?"

My headmaster and the director of admissions were horrified by the idea of me going to Columbia, although I suspect that their reasons were different from my own misgivings. Other US students had gone to Columbia, but the events of that spring must have been very difficult for the conservative US alumni and board of trustees to swallow. The headmaster felt that because I was a quiet, fairly reclusive person, I might not survive the political turmoil of Columbia. Furthermore, the strike at Columbia opened up another dilemma. For as much as they did not want me to go to Columbia, they wanted me to go to Yale and Princeton even less. They persuaded my parents that I should go to a smaller, less high-pressure place like Colgate.

I was outraged by this. I had not suffered something akin to social ostracism to go to Colgate. Moreover, I had been seduced by the gaudy display of class, wealth, and power of University School. In my own way I was deeply anxious for a piece of the power and the good life that I had seen dangled before me for two years. I was deranged by my own sense of entitlement. I knew of at least two Yale legacies who were not even in the honor society, the Cum Laude Society, to which I had recently been inducted. Moreover, before I sent in my decision to Columbia, I had been waylaid by three very mediocre, rich WASP classmates who told me to hurry up so they could find out who Yale would accept from the waiting list. I looked down my nose at these three with great adolescent self-righteousness. What demands could such privileged people ever make of me? I disdainfully thought.

I casually accepted my own judgment of how little sense my elders were making at this moment. As Mr. McKinley, the headmaster, whom I admired a great deal, went on and on, I looked out the window, seeing my dark reflection and myself as never before. Whatever my pretensions, I was—to the rest of the world, at least—indistinguishable from the overheated rabble in the black Cleveland streets. The trees, which become so gray and sere in the Cleveland winter, were beginning to green. I think there was an athletic match that day. I could see the beautiful mansions across the way. The branches on the trees were absolutely still. Across the way three middle schoolers walked slowly and elegantly. They clasped their books to their chests in a gesture learned from their elders. They were in no rush; the future was coming to them. I looked at this place and knew it was Eden, but that I had to leave. I held my ground. I got my way. We settled on Yale.

CHAPTER NINE

Two Speakers Come to Yale

My parents drove me from Cleveland to Yale. The trip took nearly twenty hours, and we arrived in New Haven late at night and exhausted. The next day, we went to the university, stopping first at the Old Campus, a quad encircled by old dormitories in which college freshman are housed.

As a Head Start worker in Glenville, my mother had seen a growing group of black radicals who floated between the government-run inner-city programs, establishing political ties, gathering information, and hoarding weapons. And finally the riots erupted. Snipers fired at the firemen from open windows in the empty decayed buildings in Hough. The next day, army Jeeps and personnel carriers patrolled the street. My mother was stopped at a National Guard checkpoint in Glenville. She cried. She and my father had come here as a young couple to start new lives. The great upheaval that had haunted their dinnertime discussions was here.

My parents, who were still shaken by the riots in Cleveland that summer, were anxious about coming to the Yale campus, and my father had wondered whether he should put on a sport coat. He was surprised to see large crowds of casual, mild-mannered parents, many in T-shirts, carrying their children's clothes in cardboard grocery store boxes to the dormitories. Surrounded by large old buildings, the Old Campus was what I imagined the Cleveland Heights High parking lot might look like on a fall Saturday afternoon during a football game. Out in the quad parents and freshmen were bargaining for old dressers, desks, and tables, which were traditionally sold by upperclassmen to the entering class. People smiled and waved to each other. They seemed happy to be in New Haven. The pleasant people I was encountering were the children of the transformation about which my class's parents at US had been warned. These suburban middle-class people were the arrivistes about whom the three mediocre US legacies had been sulking. They, a grasping bourgeoisie, had made it into the world of upper-class entitlement. A social upheaval had come here too.

I was by now used to this kind of disruption of my expectations. But I cannot say the same of my white classmates, many of whom seemed to be overwhelmed as they reckoned the difference between their expectations and reality at Yale. My classmates came to Yale rather like a group of local champions arriving at an all-state swimming meet. Yet the world that greeted them was not the world of merit but the world of privileged entitlement. At a reception given by President Kingman Brewster, we encountered a series of elegantly dressed administrators and board members. We joined a line to meet President Brewster, who greeted us by name after being prompted by an assistant. The main building of Branford College consisted of an elegant dining hall and a lounge, and at the back of the dining room was a leather-padded pit where the faculty fellows took their meals once a week. Outside was a grassy quad on which I saw two white-suited seniors playing tennis, maintaining the ball at the proper height despite the absence of a net. At the end of the first week, a party was held at Branford College for the new lowerclassmen. These parties, hosted by Master Trinkaus and his wife, would turn out to be drunken affairs at which the master's wife, a thin, provocatively dressed Frenchwoman, would stand around with a group of tall, pimpled New Yorkers who complained about studying for the Regents during their senior year. "Oh, it is just like the bac, the cruel bac," Mrs. Trinkaus would say.

This discussion gave me some pause. She had been hearing the complaints— as well as the vilely accented French—of these New York high school grads for at least the last ten years. By now these complaints must have become an early-fall ritual. Why should these new Yale students complain about the meritocratic system that got them into a major Ivy League school—what had they wanted more at Stuyvesant, Bronx High School of Science, or Brooklyn Tech than admission to Yale? The answer was a little frightening. Already after just a week, they wanted the ease and prerogative of privilege of the elite that they had displaced. In seven days they already yearned to become part of the privileged upper-class world that they beheld.

Not everyone adapted to Yale in the same way. One student dropped out after only three days—his case was much discussed, and I remember it well because he was my roommate. He was from a small rural town in Pennsylvania; his mother was an unfashionably stout woman who wore a rumpled dress, and his father, a bulky man in his fifties, dressed in corduroy pants and a plaid shirt with a large grease spot. I remember them well because when we met, both parents stared at me for a good three minutes with the kind of incredulousness that even people from Rye and Ardsley were rapidly learning to suppress in their encounters with blacks.

Even given this unpromising background, my roommate's departure was food for thought; he might have easily found other lodging if he did not want to room with a black and despite his quietness, he had loaded up on science courses in a way that showed a familiar kind of intellectual arrogance. As I grew acclimated to Yale, however, other reasons for his departure came to mind. Given his self-conscious uprightness, I suspected that he may have been frightened by the availability—indeed, the ubiquity—of drugs in our dormitory. The cache of narcotics in the entryway to Wright Hall was, even by Yale standards, something extraordinary. I had never seen a marijuana cigarette before, but by the end of my first week at Yale, I had had the opportunity to contemplate my first kilo—two plain brown shopping bags filled with something that looked like straw. The psychological dislocation caused by living amid this suburban contraband might have been intensified by the froideur, the preppy cool, with which these pharmaceutical undertakings were accepted everywhere. I was stunned at my dorm advisor's response when I asked about the legal jeopardy involved in having, by my count, ten tabs of acid in the bathroom's open medicine cabinet. A self-assured Asian American law student with a tall, leggy black girlfriend, he quietly chuckled at my question, never breaking the reserve with which Princeton graduates let midwestern Yale freshmen know just how innocent they really are. After about a month at Yale, I came to see my departed roommate as a secret sharer in my alienation, and his frightened silence as a screen on which I projected my own terror.

My own deepest terrors were sexual. Obsessed with my schoolwork, I had barely dated for two years in Cleveland Heights. However, there had been an upheaval, and during my first year in New Haven, it was clear that in the aftermath of the sexual revolution, sex was one of the fruits of victory: a period of eager reconstruction in which everyone, it seemed, was engaged. The freedom that had been won was, fantasy-like, masturbatory in its apparent gratifications. Yale was not yet coed during my first year. But sometime during my second semester, for a week the school was desegregated for visits by girls interested in Yale. I do not use the word "interested" lightly. By means unknown to me, my bedroom was commandeered by what seems to have been the most sexually active female undergraduate on the East Coast—a judgment in which I persist, despite my knowledge of how fierce the competition for that honor must have been in the spring of 1969. My memory of this week, during which I slept on the suite's living room couch, is foggy, but I remember that she somehow went through rolls and rolls of toilet paper, which I, a kind of designated eunuch, was required to bring her. I remember her vividly because in her perpetual dishabille she was clearly the fantasy-fulfilling extension of what one saw of girls from visiting schools sitting in the living rooms of our dorm suites in short plaid skirts hiked up to their thighs. Basking in the prestige of their schools—Smith, Vassar, Mount Holyoke—their faces were aglow with the casual elitism of which SAT scores of 1450, radical politics, and the carefully cultivated illusion of sexual availability were all a part. They were following a dictum announced from a high quarter. "Fuck," enjoined our resident advisor from Princeton at the end of one of his long philosophical discourses. He said it calmly, not licentiously, in the rational patrician manner with which, I supposed, the act was being performed by my classmates all around me.

During my first week at Yale, I was shocked to find that sex, which I, like most eighteen-year-olds in Cleveland Heights, had thought of as a secularized religious mystery, was really a social pleasantry. And I suspect much of the present feminist attack on the commoditization and reification of the female body may represent the return of repressed inhibitions on the part of people who now for the entire world seem to me like the girls in the living room of Wright Hall. One of my freshmen roommates loved big words, his favorite being "usufruct." Surely if the fruits of the sexual revolution were anything, that is what they were: an invitation to taste and see the carnal goodness that, like perfect teeth and trust funds, blossomed in Glen Ellyn, Shaker Heights, and Westchester County. Much is now made of date rape at the kind of small liberal arts school where I now teach, and I am shocked by how little I heard of any such violence at Yale. Indeed, sex, like drugs, was in the popular imagination balanced with a civility and work ethic leavened with upper-class understatement. I remember listening in the laundry room to the casual conversation of a couple in my class with their friends as they discussed, with characteristic wit and detachment, the girl's particularly tenacious yeast infection. Both junior-year Phi Beta Kappas who would go to law school at Yale and Harvard, they were already dressed in the polo shirts and jeans that are now de rigueur in the expensive color photographs of class reunions in the *Yale Alumni Magazine*. Once the girl wore velvet hot pants as a complicated camp joke—an haut bourgeois send-up of lower-class tastes.

Perhaps the most unexpected part of the democratic revolution at Yale was the blacks. The white middle class had barely recognized the upheaval in its own lives before it noticed the presence of blacks. The riots that devastated inner-city Hough and Glenville had been a year late. In 1967, roughly 120 American inner cities had burned. Power is holy in American life, and I suspect the sheer force yielded by blacks in the previous two years had earned them the grim respect of the white populace. The parents of my classmates looked and waved politely at my family—far more politely than they would four years later when they began to perceive affirmative action as a threat to their welfare. Moreover, there was, during my early years at Yale, a fascination with the black presence as part of the brave new world that had arrived.

The collegiate apartheid sanctioned by those who rejected similar arrange-ments in South Africa had already found a home at Yale in 1970. No less a personage than John P. Trinkaus, an eminent biologist and the master of my college, would shock me with a defense of the reconstructed color line at post-integration Yale. In this new order, according to him, blacks had achieved an admirable autonomy that, to his mind at least, was a pleasing change from the mind-set of those earlier unctuous Negroes who would do anything to get ahead in the academic, political, and social worlds of Yale.

Any black student seeking to avoid black Yale could do so by refusing to sit at the black tables in the residential colleges or on the commons. If one got into this habit during one's freshmen year, one could avoid the whole contingent, only to encounter them years later in the late seventies as partners in major law firms, vice presidents of banks, and doctors in the *Yale Alumni Magazine* like a partially forgotten dream.

I sometimes unexpectedly found myself identified as a Yale student on the basis of my color. At a mixer in Northampton, a slender Smithie dressed in the already outdated style of Haight-Ashbury—flowery skirt, boots, and all—im-mediately recognized me as a Yalie, citing my skin color as evidence. Seeing my horror, she told me I would never make it through the night if I didn't learn to drink more. I saw her a few times afterward, and I must say that I learned from her wit. It was impossible for a black to avoid being taken for a devotee of black culture. Any African American, that is, would inevitably be assumed to be black, a statement that perhaps meant something different in the late sixties than it does now.

Blackness was not only beautiful but attractive in a way that I had never seen it before. Our philosophy teacher Professor Fogelin, lecturing brilliantly on Plato, Spinoza, and Nietzsche, spoke in passing about the black power salute given by the two African American track champions at the 1968 Olympics. He said this solemnly, with a deep gratitude—wholly without irony.

What was most puzzling to me about the separatism of the period was the utter similarity between the blacks and whites who kept the greatest distance from each other. To a certain extent this similarity was recognized, as it inevitably had to be, when so many blacks I considered to be separatists were tapped for senior societies. As a high school senior I had read E. Franklin Frazier's *The Black Bourgeoisie* in the hypnotic reverie in which all great books about America placed me. Frazier argued that the black middle class had created a play world that was completely imitative of bourgeois white society. In retrospect this was very close to correct; however, the black bourgeoisie suddenly seemed, in all its anti-intellectualism, to be really in the game now, playing with a skill and cynicism that made their white counterparts look as politically and sexually impotent as the sassy roughness of Aretha Franklin's voice hinted they were.

Social integration, it soon became clear, was for the very few blacks who had managed to wedge their way into the school's academic and social elites, and people like me who did not know their place. I was and am forever being reminded of this, most recently at an academic colloquium where Armstead Robinson, then a full professor at the University of Virginia, boasted that he and his friends at Yale had created the Ghetto, an all-black dormitory. How, he asked plaintively, could the son of a Negro minister from Kansas City live with Andover graduates? I was deeply moved, for my parents were certainly not socially prominent enough to consort with any of the established black ministers in Cleveland. And it occurred to me for the first time that for all the social baggage of my lower-middle-class background, I was free of the particular status-related anxieties borne by the truly middle- and upper-middle-class blacks educated in largely black environments. It was an oft-repeated joke in my household that, compared to our relations who were doctors, lawyers, and college administrators, we had no status. Indeed, our only redemption was the fact that blacks, whatever their pretensions, had no real status or power anywhere in American society. But for the authentic black bourgeoisie, who have never been in on this joke, the disappearance of the established hallmarks of black life (the fraternities, the various rituals) must have been devastating indeed. In retrospect, the black student organizations, the informally designated all-black dining-room tables, and even much of the militant demand for African American studies courses were attempts of a middle class to create a presence for itself in what they saw, in perhaps the deepest irony of ironies, to be a cultural wasteland. Seen in this light, the accomplishment of these shrewd young blacks was remarkable; they manufactured the simulacrum of culture and political power negotiable in the counsels of the most distinguished universities of the land.

I remember reading an article in the *Yale Alumni Magazine* in which a well-known black leader questioned the relevance of sixteenth-century art to African American students. Elsewhere in the article, another leader worried in a self-satisfied way about the difficulties of balancing his three-piece suit with a black consciousness. At the time I dismissed these concerns as a vulgar anti-intellectualism that had no place at a university. The attack on Italian Renaissance art demonstrated not only obscene ignorance but also poisonous contempt for the humanist values of individualism that the Renaissance represented. These people, I raged to anyone who would listen, knew their real enemies—the central philosophical and moral traditions of the West.

There was something special about the ease with which black cultural nationalism, with all its repressions, came to serve the therapeutic needs of an emerging middle class displaced from its traditional centers of socialization. It was no accident that my college years coincided with the age of the ego, the most recent triumph of the therapeutic ideal. Like their wealthy white counterparts, black students had grasped the role of culture as a means to ego gratification.

Whatever radical sympathies I brought to Yale were destroyed by the 1970 Mayday protest during Huey Newton's trial in New Haven. I had entered Yale with a cynical view of privileged white radical students as well as contempt for the black middle class. This attitude not only contributed to endless confusion but ultimately made me a deeply alienated loner. My growing sense of estrangement came to a head during the apocalyptic protests at Yale during the time of the Cambodian invasion.

All the derangements of the drug culture, the free-floating paranoia of the New Left, and the R&B fantasies of the nascent black power movement coalesced during a week whose neurotic tone simply amplified the dominant tenor of Yale life. Indeed, for all the supposed political significance of the time, what I remember most was its ethos of manic depression: a roller coaster of highs and lows. At one meeting of students and faculty in the hockey arena, I saw the eminent psychologist Kenneth Keniston rise from the crowd to introduce himself as a psychologist and lead a demented speaker off the podium. Watching this bizarre spectacle, I felt a certain amount of ironic detachment at seeing the author of *The Uncommitted* confront the public manifestation of his academic specialty. As a senior in high school, I had read and admired Keniston's subtle case study of Inburn. Although as an eighteen-year-old I could not grasp the book's import completely, it did alert me to the fact that the casual postures of alienation assumed with so much effort in Cleveland Heights might not in and of themselves be a good thing. The study of Inburn, whom Keniston, in a typically literary gesture, compares to Ishmael, reminded me of a much more raffish good friend of mine who would never gain the attention of Keniston's Harvard students. However, here on the stage on that spring night was deep alienation, and Keniston was approaching the podium with all the distaste of a professor asked to apply one of his more abstract theories to a real-life problem. My sense of detachment deepened as I watched him look around the audience in search, I now surmise, of the photographer from the *New York Times.*

The depressing self-importance of one's elders could surpass the ubiquitous mania of the Yale students. As I walked with a large crowd to the hockey arena that night, I'd heard a young student casually correct in thick chino pants, blue button-down oxford, and a beige London Fog jacket recite Yeats's "September 1919." I didn't recognize him as an English major, but he looked very literary, rather like the tall disdainful prep student who'd announced outside my advisor's office that he would not take Harold Bloom's seminar because he so disliked the riffraff that gathered around these "great men." The oxford-clad student spoke the words of the poem loudly and a trifle too quickly, with the intentionally unpremeditated earnestness that plays such a large part of Yalie charm. As his lockjaw accent floated over the crowd moving in the evening darkness down the hill to the rink, one could almost forgive him for imposing upon a crowd of three hundred in order to impress the haughty-looking blonde girl beside him. It has taken me twenty years to realize that that student's arrogant exhilaration, altogether a match for Keniston's somber self-importance, was what that night was really about.

To thrive in chaos, to impose the order of the self upon the disorder of change, was the great lesson of Yale in the late sixties and early seventies. And to my hardened sensibility, the order of the self meant the arrogant privilege of the most self-dramatizing of my classmates. As my professors strained to show how Pope and Milton drew upon the antinomies of *concordia discors* to dramatize the order within the divinely created plenitude celebrated in poems like "Windsor-Forest" and *Paradise Lost,* so were my classmates forever imposing the demands of their imperial egos upon the vast resources represented by Yale's intellectual, cultural, and material magnificence, which may have been the closest thing to the sacred that they knew. Indeed, one quickly came to feel that the scholarly concerns inside the classroom and the uncontrollable appetites for diverse experience without were part of the autumnal ripeness of late-sixties American prosperity and of the imperial order that sustained that wealth. The drive to take it all in may well have been a farewell gesture to financial reserves that would rapidly disappear as gas prices rose and stagflation emerged. Certainly no English major at Yale could fail to connect the perpetual suburban version of *The Tempest* being performed on campus and the megalomania that emerged when the Black Panthers came to New Haven for the trial of Huey Newton, when rumors of the impending apocalyptic destruction of Yale spread throughout those parochial academic communities of the East Coast. For all its references to the Book of Apocalypse, this heated period was merely one of the final scenes of the long, expensive performance of living theater at the center of upper-class liberal life in the sixties.

A sense of apocalypse was very much in the air, as one might expect of a student community anticipating the arrival of the Black Panthers while swaying to the beat of the Doors. Much was made of the way in which the Yale community pulled together to save itself that weekend from impending disaster. The school had shut down its facilities, and a crowd gathered for demonstrations. In disgust (and fear), I abandoned New Haven. Much has been made of the hardships of portable toilets and the granola eaten by all after the dining room closed. That week, I rode down to La Guardia and took a plane to Cleveland. As I was walking to the hotel limousine in New Haven on my way to La Guardia and the Midwest, I saw the family of a classmate. Apparently his younger brother just arrived from the family's uptown co-op on Park Avenue for the adventure. The mother, still slender in her forties, was dressed in a linen summer suit. She stepped out of the new Volvo station wagon to kiss her younger son, dramatically putting both hands around his face: a publicly conspicuous display of concern clearly intended as a political statement. I was not moved. Indeed, I was totally disgusted, and the stuffed briefcase I carried with materials for papers on Stevens and Eliot was my answer to the upper-class Babylon in the dorms that I was beginning to despise, as well as to the gentrified Armageddon at hand. This revulsion welled throughout the upper part of my body, and I would not realize its source until years later when Nancy Helmbold, my Latin teacher at the University of Chicago, asked me to translate the words—although they were appearing in another context— "Carthago delenda est." When I returned to Yale after a weekend in Cleveland, however, I found not John of the Apocalypse but, quite predictably, Rabelais. Upon my return, I was met by a close friend who informed me that in the heat of a spring night, a couple had copulated nude on one of the green billiard tables in the basement of Branford College. Whether or not it happened was, of course, beside the point, the luridness of the rumor itself being the logical fulfillment of the erotic exhibitionism that was never far from the center of leftist politics in the sixties. Yet even the friend who reported this to me—a smart, witty gay student of comparative literature—seemed a little taken aback. There was an unsettling hint of derangement in the idea underlying the tale itself; even if the event had transpired as alleged, public intercourse was not the kind of behavior one traditionally expected from upper-class heterosexuals. The image of a world turned upside down would predominate my memories of the week that followed, the most vivid of which was the sight of excrement smeared onto a piece of paper on one of the bulletin boards of the college post office. Understandably, perhaps, this crude allusion to the fashionable doctrine that the medium is the message provoked no excitement. Standing in a nearby corner, I watched out of curiosity as student after student passed it without even turning to find the source of the smell.

I retreated to the library in the following years. There I spent most of my time reading whatever looked interesting. I did well enough to graduate cum laude with honors in English. But to tell the truth, I was far too traumatized by the cultural and sexual derangements of the academy to concentrate all my energy on schoolwork as I previously had. And I must say that after schoolwork, my major activity at Yale was combing the stacks in Sterling Memorial Library at night and reading my find in the huge stuffed chairs of the Linonia and Brothers Reading Room, surrounded by the refreshingly nun-like graduate students who favored long woolen skirts, gray stockings, and plain low-heeled shoes.

I had few friends. One was a tall lanky fellow from South Dakota who, by the kind of serendipity so common at Yale, had won a scholarship to a prep school in Wales, where he had excelled in math and physics, only to give up science first, and philosophy later. Late in his career at Yale, he finally gravitated to Chaucer, Whitman, and Frost. In the spring we would take long walks at two or three in the morning to East Rock through leafy green neighborhoods where Yale students are now routinely mugged. Looking up at the sky one night, he recited Robert Frost's "Canis Major":

The great Overdog,
That heavenly beast
With a star in one eye,
Gives a leap in the east.

He dances upright
All the way to the west
And never once drops
On his forefeet to rest.

I'm a poor underdog,
But tonight I will bark
With the great Overdog
That romps through the dark.[1]

We would finish up at about four at a Dunk'n Donuts that stayed open all night. I set my alarm clock to wake me up at eleven (by then I scheduled my classes late in morning and early in the afternoon), and he would return to a deeply carnal entanglement with his girlfriend. My other friends were my roommates, the sons of successful Jewish academics and businesspeople, who were unfailingly kind to me. In the spring, we occasionally spent weekends at one roommate's summer house in East Hampton, hunting clams, making chowder, and riding the father's cabin cruiser back to the small harbor, guided through the fog by the green glow of radar. I had never drunk Cointreau, seen a Long Island summer home, smelled the Sound, or eaten raw oysters culled from the Sound's shallows with a rake. The father's girlfriend was a distinguished writer and editor of children's books, and one spring at a dinner party I met a crowd of New York literati. The girlfriend, a lovely, cultivated, genteel woman, donned a slouchy cap made of blue jeans, attire of the sort favored by Yale radicals, for the occasion. Much of the conversation turned on whether or not the film *Easy Rider* was the American epic for my generation—a view I then rejected but that is of course true in ways that are painful to admit. The room was filled with a number of female editors at publishing houses, some flushing with contempt at a lecherous psychiatrist in town to promote a very successful self-help book—"nothing but a hick midwestern shrink," I heard one say between clenched teeth. And late at night I fell into a long conversation about Proust with the most diminutive of these editors, a smart, quiet woman with a slight British accent. Tom Wolfe, of course, was already wreaking great havoc among these people and their ways, but even he in much of his criti-

---

1. "Canis Major," from the book THE POETRY OF ROBERT FROST, edited by Edward Connery Lathem. Copyright 1928, 1929 by Henry Holt and Company, copyright 1956 by Robert Frost. Reprinted by permission of Henry Holt and Company, LLC.

cism could not—as very few American writers, beginning with Henry James, cannot—resist the charms of the distinctively American romance of earned wealth, possibility, and hope: the romance of Manhattan art collectors such as Robert and Ethel Scull, then celebrated by Tom Wolf as "Ethel and Spike." The luminous civility of these people who, in a kind of Weimar–New England high-mindedness, could celebrate even the children who sought to overturn them made up my most pleasant memories of Yale.

As a typically precocious reader during my first two years at Yale, I had cut my teeth on the notion of alienation long before I read central texts such as *The Economic and Philosophic Manuscripts of 1844*. In the school of ego psychology that flourished at Yale around people like Kenneth Keniston and Robert J. Lifton, this word could, in books like *The Uncommitted,* describe mildly pathological middle-class disorder. It took me a long time to discover that the alienation described by Keniston could be incredibly unsettling when experienced in real life. These notions provided in some sense the framework within which I sought to understand myself. And I suspect this language constituted such a framework for other blacks. Indeed, I was fascinated by the way in which the therapeutic language of ego, identity, and autonomy was penetrating the discourse of cultural nationalists who styled themselves as at odds with the West. That these people should pick up an essentially middle-class American ego psychology while they were supposedly rebelling against its strong hold was a deep and suggestive irony that revealed a great deal to me. For all his German refugee roots, Erikson's scheme of development seemed deeply American in its optimistic insistence on an identity that stemmed from the adaption of an autonomous ego to historical circumstances. And indeed much of the highly selective exploration by my black peers into historical figures such as Malcolm X seemed like nothing more than a kind of quest for identity and selfhood through historical reflection.

The search for a black identity was, it seemed to me, a distinctly middle-class search for those who must have the autonomy required for survival in a competitive liberal social order that devalued attachments of kinship, social status, religious affiliation, and (ironically) ethnicity. In relationship to the black masses that had not successfully moved into this social order exemplified by corporations and political institutions, black identity seemed to be a far less serious and relatively symbolic question. But in the university, questions of identity concerning notions of blackness and whiteness as they were identified with the psychological trauma of black students in a newly integrated white school were very quickly raised. This was certainly true at Yale. No criticism of another black made by an African American was more damning than the suggestion that the person in question thought he was white—always assuming the connection of identity to a racial essence. What was at stake, it seemed to me, was not so much a revolutionary consciousness but a therapeutic resolution of the deep problems that the derangements of Yale in the sixties and seventies presented for nearly everyone there.

I, of course, was suffering too and was beginning to see that the literary estrangements examined by the local luminaries and celebrated in my cultural heroes—Joyce, Dostoevsky, and Thoreau—were not always the psychological resource they seemed but something far more serious. Real alienation was loneliness, and the encounter with the inner emptiness created by that isolation. I have a particularly vivid memory of an issue of the *New Journal* that featured a series of photographs of the various greens at Yale taken from windows on days when the quads were absolutely empty. I immediately recognized these pictures as what one saw from the dorm and classroom windows when all of Yale was at a game or at a gala celebration. The pictures of the green spoke to me, in a typically literary Yale allusion, of the tremendous emptiness experienced by outsiders at a school for insiders. This association is not one made by mentally healthy undergraduates. By the time I made it, I was so horrified by my classmates' contempt for and suspicions of me that I traveled mostly by way of the underground tunnels in my residential college. My quest for any kind of organized camaraderie had long since given out.

I left the staff of the *New Journal* in shame and of my own volition when a talk I was asked to give about Gramsci failed. I am now an English professor with a PhD from an elite American university and consequently know what I should have said. A little more emphasis on Gramsci's conception of hegemonic language, perhaps as it entraps me as a black, would have done the trick. Dwelling on Gramsci's stay in prison was the wrong thing to do. A number of the editors of the journal went on to become successful academics and writers. But of course the culture game in which they were engaged had little to do with real learning. To be sure, it was a venerable cultural game grounded in the best modernist traditions—Eliot, Joyce, and Beckett—but the notion that these preppy leftists could create anything but the most shallow semblance of alienation, estrangement, and oppression was perhaps the deepest article of faith at Yale, the belief that life, any life, could imitate art. The alienation that increasingly isolated me in the library, the leather-padded pit behind the dining room, and the racing track on the roof of the gym was true estrangement, the closest to the thing itself that I ever felt or saw at Yale, and not a posture. And that relentless gnawing emptiness that I felt in what was for me the crowded desolation of Yale's campus was perhaps my first premonition of what it means to be a black in American society.

Of course, this kind of isolation and paranoia is the price paid by many blacks in many kinds of institutions. My deepest shock of recognition came when I read a *New York Times Magazine* article in which the distinguished psychologist the late Kenneth Clark said he was as paranoid as any other black academic. At Yale I came to realize that my presence in the academy violated the deepest taboo in American life, the racial boundary hedged around the American life of the mind. I suspect that one reason for the easy white acceptance of black radicalism at Yale was the cultural nationalists' profound allegiance to this deeply American article of faith. Entering the brave new world of Yale, many of the shrewd blacks of my generation promised, with few and honorable exceptions, not to violate the established intellectual turfs—indeed, to create their own—and they were therefore welcomed. I certainly felt the hint of this taboo in the eyes that lifted around me every time I found a Miltonic allusion in Wordsworth's *Prelude,* a dramatic irony in a Joyce story, or a pattern of sound and sense in Donne. Like all scholarship boys, I took my hard-earned education much more seriously than those who had acquired it from their parents' table talk. But there was something more at stake here. If blacks needed to immerse themselves in black culture for their emotional and psychological well-being, then I was engaged in a fundamentally unhealthy activity.

Of course my reading of the situation is dramatic. And one of the deepest lessons of Yale for all—white or black—is that somewhere on campus there is someone afflicted with your predicament ninefold. This person, of course, has mastered your conundrums much better than you ever shall. The knowledge that one is never off the continuum of personal, intellectual, or cultural eccentricity of course gives Yale its dizzying éclat. And I, of course, saw people carrying off the difficult balancing act in which I was engaged. Indeed, one saw fairly frequently blacks who carried the ethos of integration past a social envelope where I could not breathe. I could never initiate conversations with these people about their experiences; in fact, such conversations seemed altogether anathema to them. I was as anathema to them as the people in the Black Student Alliance were to me. One such fellow was the best student in my English 25 class. He mastered the task of close reading long before I and went on to become a very good student of Italian, German, and French, finally getting a Rhodes Scholarship and studying at Oxford. I see from the alumni directory that he is now a law professor. He was, apparently, a very good fencer and would occasionally come to my dorm to talk with another member of the Yale team, a nondescript fellow with the kind of British accent that a certain kind of student at Collegiate acquires in England to cover up his parents' Brooklynese. He was very jovial with his fellow fencers, exemplifying the kind of camaraderie at Yale I had expected from the beautifully illustrated school catalogs. But on the street, walking alone when I saw him, he looked businesslike, efficient, and more than a little grim. He never said more than two or three words to me despite my attempts to engage him in conversation. When I moved into the all-black dormitory my senior year, I found that none of the black students knew this fellow. I envied him deeply—he had made his separate peace with Yale and kept his balance on what I increasingly saw as a psychological high-wire act.

Very little of the psychiatric counseling that I got at Yale was useful. Indeed, most of my sessions with the earnest young residents I encountered now remind me of *New Yorker* cartoons, which may have been the great original of the experience in the mind of doctor and patient alike. One young psychiatrist, a tall black, encouraged me to attend the Black Student Alliance meetings and become involved with my African American peers. He ferociously attacked the claims I made for my parents' wisdom and accused me of making myself odd out of pure perversity. Our sessions stopped after he cut off all his hair and donned a gold earring. Seeing him at our last session looking for all the world like Kareem Abdul-Jabbar in a tweed coat, I signed off. He may have been fighting his own demons. Year later I learned that he had committed suicide. My most successful therapist asked me about myself, looked at my academic record, bluntly asked me what I expected from life, and made me wait a month before I saw him again. After a month I seized the glimmer of sanity he seemed to be holding out to me and told him that things could not be as bad as I thought. My doctor praised me for coming to my senses and we said good-bye.

During my final year at Yale, I joined the "black entryway," an all-black unit of suites situated around a single stairwell in a gesture of therapeutic goodwill. I made enemies for life there, but the surface of my daily existence calmed rather as water will under oil. I met a number of black graduate students whom I still count as some of the brightest people I have ever known. Two were law students, one of whom, a woman named Susan, informed me that she wished to run a boutique. If the development of a sense of humor is a sign of mental health, I was getting well. Perfectly charmed, I followed her everywhere, flirting with her as she flirted with other law students, to the dismay and amusement of my male law school friend, who prefaced an invitation to any event with a sly "Susan's gonna be there." I also met a black graduate student from Spelman and experienced my first encounter with the utter scorn poured by black alumni of predominantly Negro colleges upon black Ivy Leaguers. Some of my roommates from the entryway were in a class she taught; fortunately I was not, and I had the benefit of her abundantly witty observations on Yale.

I continued hanging out with my friend from South Dakota, who congratulated me on my newfound peace of mind. For the first time, too, I began to take an interest in the many distinguished people who came to speak at Yale—and a stunning lot they were. On one Parnassian night I heard Telford Taylor, Eugene Rostow, Noam Chomsky, a famous professor at Yale Law whose name I do not remember, and an even more anonymous middle-aged philosophy professor from CCNY who charmed the audience with reminders of his utter insignificance in this distinguished company. This brilliant panel spoke on the subject of war crimes, each speaker seemingly more brilliant than the last. The glow of the highly burnished arguments is all that remains long after the actual subject matter has dissipated in the course of twenty years.

More accessible to me intellectually, because of my interests and reading, were other events. One was a poetry reading given by Robert Lowell. He appeared there elegantly dressed in a tweed coat and regimental tie, his high forehead wreathed by graying hair. By 1972, he was already a canonical figure. He walked slowly, spoke in measured tones, and gave every sign of the exhaustion that one might expect from his disordered personal life. He made a brief joke about the Harvard-Yale football rivalry only to conclude somberly that he put no stock in that kind of thing, none at all. Already in the Indian summer of his intellectual eminence, Lowell at that moment possessed enormous personal dignity.

I remember that the crowd was full of not only the literary types one saw at this kind of gathering but also the seedily dressed radicals. I suspect most of them were there because of Lowell's fame in the antiwar movement, celebrated in Norman Mailer's *The Armies of the Night*. I had read this book during one of the summers I spent working as a janitor and groundskeeper at the apartment building owned by a wealthy friend's father, and even then I was struck by the sociological shrewdness of Mailer's commentary. Mailer's praise stressed the conservative aspects of Lowell's character and career; the poet's family connections extending through the Lowells and Winslows made everything he wrote seem instantly a part of American history. Moreover, Lowell's sexual and psychological derangements—of which that audience was probably aware—as

well as the first part of "Waking Sunday Morning" made him a very real contemporary for upper-class radicals living with their girlfriends on Elavil. The
heavy burdens of fame, Harvard affectations, and medication that made his
shoulders stooped and blurred his speech were in the end a reassuring sanction
to all who felt that their parentally subsidized roads of excess might lead to a
similar palace of wisdom. Lowell's poetic fame and his appeal to that audience,
I imagine, probably stemmed from his ability to wear the cultural, sexual, and
psychological traumas of the late-sixties upper class so well.

I was one of only two black students out of the nearly two hundred in the
room where Lowell spoke. I knew this fellow from a special seminar for the
intensive English major, English 89. We may have nodded, but I don't think we
spoke. I noticed him searching for a willowy brunette classmate who favored
T-shirts and short skirts. In class she talked brilliantly about the stylistic details
of French texts and expressed herself through a series of histrionic gestures that
never ceased to impress me. Once after making a point, she leaned forward,
put a cigarette to her lips, and spread her arms on the table. I stared at her,
stunned, while the teacher glared at me, grunted, and lit her cigarette.

I must say that I looked for another black only out of idle habit. Whenever my
family went to the art museum, my mother was given to vehemently denouncing
the black middle class for its absence from these institutions. I did not share her
outrage, but she aroused my curiosity. Remembering her anger, it occurred to
me that in the enlightened seventies no one would mind the absence of blacks,
even at the reading of so acclaimed an American poet as Lowell. My English
teacher in English 89, who was fond of the echo's great original in *Hamlet*, might
ask what Lowell was to them or they to Lowell. Were not the blacks engaged
in the creation of a new culture? Their absence was not a cultural omission but
the necessary consequence of their having other fish to fry.

I do not remember whether Lowell read "Waking Sunday Morning" at this
reading; I suspect he did. But I cannot think of this reading without remembering this wonderfully Horatian poem. Lowell's poetry as he grew older could
often be the creature of his moodiness, and the first poem of this sequence
was, of course, a meditation whose meanings were buoyed along the tides of
sexual exuberance, reflection, sorrow, and somber acceptance. I cannot think
of my seminar leader in English 89, already a close reader's close reader, without distinguishing the way in which this poem divides between good and bad
leisure in temporary retirement from public life: the speaker onboard a yacht
pondering the inevitable stain of life as opposed to Lyndon Johnson surrounded
by his speechwriters in the pool. But more to the point for me and the age in

which I live was the political meditation of the retired poet who still wishes to speak to his age's men of action.

I can't now think of this poem without thinking of my ride on my classmate's cabin cruiser back to port in the dense gray fog of Long Island Sound. What did such a ride have to do with my parents in Cleveland Heights, their black church, and the people they encountered daily in Hough, Glenville, and Wade Park? Lowell's imagery of an elegant move down to the sea in a ship was of course not only literary but a scene from a privileged family of wealth and reputation made possible by appropriated, not earned, wealth. This was the kind of wealth possessed by my Yale classmates, their parents, and of course Yale itself. My appreciation of the poem was made possible by appropriated wealth not earned: the fruit of benevolent patronage not unlike that doled out to me by the Ford Foundation in the sixties. As I reflected on the poem, it began to hold out the possibility of a leisurely but politicized voice, the kind of voice that Yale might give another privileged descendant of slaves.

Lowell's message was a tragic one, but it was tempered by an upper-class stoic optimism. Great civilizations—Greece, Rome, and England—had risen and fallen in the past. And such would rise and fall again. The waning of America in the late sixties was itself part of an organic process, the altogether typical life of an imperial civilization. The best and most accomplished societies would decline, their best and most sophisticated poets urbanely bidding them farewell. The decadence I raged against at Branford College was, like the war in Vietnam, part of the inevitable mortality of any social order, and Lowell's quiet, firm voice urged that civilized men in such societies have always accepted this. For all its horror, Lowell's view was a deeply civilizing one and, in its pointed elitism, a rather reassuring one.

There was much talk in the late sixties and early seventies about relevance and the emptiness of tradition. But I suspect that Lowell's presence was valued so much in the period by many young, mostly white, people because he brought the deep consolations of classical literary tradition to the tumultuous present. He was a citizen of learning who treated his fellow inhabitants on the page and at public literary events with enormous grace and deference. He allowed the most present-minded radicals to accept the traumatic turmoil of the day as part of the human condition and, in doing so, offered them a deeply humanistic identity, although they often spurned its terms. Speaking to his audience at Yale, he implicitly affirmed the academy, then under fierce attack, as a place where art, politics, and youth might not only coexist but thrive.

Another significant memory of my senior year at Yale was a panel discussion with Kenneth Clark, Martin Kilson, and a young black professor from the law school. The evening of the event began auspiciously. My residential college hosted a cocktail party for Clark and Kilson, the two honored guests. As was the custom, a lottery was held to select those who would attend the cocktail party. All the winners were black although there were surely other white contestants. I was particularly excited; my two black friends in the law school had decided to come, and more important, I would get to see Kenneth Clark. I had grown up with very few heroes, and Clark was one of them. I had read *Dark Ghetto* for a freshman sociology paper on urban black life and, more to the point, I don't recall a day during my last five years in Cleveland when I did not see a copy of *Prejudice and Your Child* on my mother's chest of drawers.

My mother was aware of Clark's argument that segregation had an extremely destructive effect on black children's psychological development. Of course this doctrine was, for as long as I can remember, contested in my day-to-day experience. During my senior year, I went out for walks with my graduate student friend from Spelman, who was already bemoaning the destruction of extremely effective black schools in the South under desegregation policies.

I remained deeply sympathetic to Clark. His view suggested the really deep fears and anxieties one sensed in the black middle-class students who were increasingly choosing to sit at separate tables at lunch and live in segregated dorms. I was living in such a dorm my senior year. There I discovered no black nirvana but found the black middle class to be as boisterous, parochial, and nervous as I had ever known it in Cleveland. On Clark's analysis, these young people were doing themselves permanent psychological damage by legitimizing white society's claims to their inferiority. Whatever one thought of Clark, his work on school desegregation, ghetto life, and American institutions garnered him preeminence in his field. He would later become the president of the American Psychological Association. Paradoxically, he was, like Kilson, the very model of the engaged black intellectual. Unlike many of his nationalist opposition, Clark had actually taught in black schools, played an important role in desegregation cases, and contributed major works of scholarship. He was part of a distinguished tradition of African American social scientists that already included the likes of E. Franklin Frazier, Charles Johnson, Allison Davis, and Oliver Cox. At that moment in the early seventies at Yale, it was impossible not to see him as their legitimate successor.

Clark, a slender, elegantly dressed man, came into the master's home in the residential college and quickly retreated to a corner of the room, where he stood with a very light-skinned, curly-haired law student and his white girlfriend. I had not seen many blacks with such light skin (as I would when I became an instructor at Howard) and did not realize that this fellow was black until a classmate revealed this to me. Anyway, this light-skinned fellow had managed to carve out an intellectually and socially vital life outside the de facto segregation at Branford College at Yale, and he seemed no worse for the wear. As far as I could tell, he was a friendly guy; I rather liked and admired him.

Clark's actions then went unnoticed—they would be recalled with some force later that night—largely because of Kilson, who was busily engaged in dialogue with a crowd of black students around him. Kilson was a political scientist well known for his well-received first book on Sierra Leone, *Political Change in a West African State.* In the late sixties and early seventies, he would distinguish himself as a commentator on African American political, social, and intellectual life in general. When I got to the University of Chicago, I would read two superb essays of his on black student militancy in the British literary magazine *Encounter.* He was a member of the editorial boards of *American Scholar* and *Dissent,* as well as a firm opponent of the war in Vietnam who could not be intimidated by the infantile Left. The novelist Julian Mayfield, a colleague of mine at Howard, knew Kilson in Ghana, where both were part of a group of émigrés that included W. E. B. Du Bois. "Black people," Julian liked to say, "would never do anything that satisfied Martin Kilson." But Julian had a self-educated man's grim admiration for the fact that Kilson never got his facts wrong or sullied the logic of his fiercely made interpretations.

At a signal moment in the conversation, Kilson claimed that there was no major black professor of English in America, but even then it seemed like an extraordinary claim. A slender black economics major pointed to the presence of Arna Bontemps, who was then in residence at Yale. Bontemps, Kilson sniffed, was no academic; he was a mere man of letters. This was exactly the right distinction, I thought, but not many people would have dared to have made it at that moment. Kilson was self-righteous, but he was also at ease. He gossiped casually with the graduate students about their common acquaintances, once drifting into an explosive argument with a friend of mine concerning the teaching competence of his Nobel Prize–winning chemistry professor at UCLA. "Just what were your law boards?" Kilson asked. Kilson had taken a lot of heat from black student militants at Harvard. When I got to the University of Chicago, a Harvard alumnus, black of course, boasted to me that he and his friends had made Kilson's life miserable. But despite the fierce controversy and sometimes hatred that swirled around Harvard's first black tenured professor, he never lost the university wit's love of give-and-take; indeed, he never lost his love of the university.

At dinner, Kilson and Clark held forth. Clark was clearly disgusted by the all-black company he had encountered in the master's hall. From the head of the table came a string of obviously interpreted and reinterpreted comments that were attributed mostly to Clark. Did we know that our white liberal teachers gave us A's and B's to keep us out of their faces? Could we imagine how much lower our board scores were than those of our white colleagues? A black professor then at Yale was, one heard, dismissed by the two visiting luminaries as mere window dressing. My friend the law student told Clark's secretary that a man of Clark's distinction should have been embarrassed to have behaved in such a way. The secretary shrugged helplessly.

By the time dinner was finished and the two had taken their place at the podium, at least Clark's intentions were clear. Both had taken enormous amounts of abuse from student radicals in the past few years, and tonight the tables were turned. Clark began with a grandiloquently sarcastic reference to Yale's distinguished halls. Kilson, shortly afterward, was moved to remark (with a sarcasm missed by most in the audience) that Lincoln University, his alma mater (the school of Thurgood Marshall, Kwame Nkrumah, Langston Hughes, and Horace Mann Bond, to mention only the most distinguished), had been last in the academic procession.

Both Clark and Kilson spoke briefly of the dim prospects for blacks in the technological era. Later they fielded questions. There were some of the predictably long polemical questions from the cultural nationalists who had drifted in as the night wore on. These fellows loved to intimidate visiting black middle-class academics with the gestures and rhetoric of black power, derogating their Uncle Tom–ishness and sycophancy. This, of course, was what Kilson and Clark had anticipated all along. Kilson was direct and blunt, delivering an eloquent attack on black anti-intellectualism. Clark, aloof, distinguished, with a nearly tragic haughtiness, asked of one incoherent questioner, "Do I have to answer this?" his forehead creasing with the weariness of having answered a hundred such questions at a hundred events such as this. Clark, in answer to an earnest inquiry about blacks' chances of surviving, answered as Sterling Brown might have answered, although without Brown's tragic optimism. Blacks would survive, Clark said, as they always had: through the mother wit of the folk tradition. He said this with a bitter smile.

CHAPTER TEN

Crack-Up

During the summer following my graduation from Yale I had what I shall call a collapse. I came home to the large house in the suburb of Forest Hills that my parents had recently bought after nearly thirty years in Cleveland. After their long sojourn through the city's urban wilderness, they had acquired a sense of humor about the troubles they had seen. At the back of our brick house, they built a large green closed-in porch. After my father hosed the driveway on Saturday, he sat on a leather lounge chair in the porch, listening to Gershwin or Mozart. On Sunday mornings, he and my mother argued over the black models who were beginning to appear in the fashion supplements of the *New York Times Magazine*. "Little thugs," he would say of the slender young dark boys who now flaunted Fila and Polo pants in spring pictorials meant for the rich people from Shaker Heights and Forest Hills about to head out to St. Martaan on holiday. My mother would remonstrate, perhaps about black identity, but he wouldn't be listening; I suspect he was searching his pockets for candy. "Rapists," he would snort. I presumed that he had long known that he had nothing to learn on the subject of who the white folks now thought he was.

I began my usual summer job at Sherri Park, an imposing apartment complex in Beachwood owned by my prep school friend Les Wolf's father and named after Les's sister. I spent most of my time cutting lawns, removing garbage, and cleaning empty apartments. I worked hard there. Elderly Jewish ladies awaited my arrival with the summer flowers; sometimes they brought me orange juice and bagels as I weeded the yard. Every morning I rode the No. 32 bus with the black maids from the inner city out to Cleveland Heights and Mayfield Heights, and farther into Beachwood. They chattered in broad southern and northern urban dialects at the back of the bus. I occasionally turned to look at them. The contrast between this and the hopeful conversations I had heard during Communion in the pews at Antioch Baptist Church among black women wearing their employer's cast-off frocks was a little unsettling. The experience raised questions about where I myself was going, and one day upon returning home, I put my khaki uniform in the laundry room and decided to do nothing. I crawled into bed and read until I tired of that. Distraught for no reason, I simply refused to get up.

Over and over again I repeated the name of a girl I had known at Yale like a mantra. I refused to go to my job. Probably suspecting me of loafing around, my parents investigated with the disinterestedness that they generally brought to my complaints about work. Looking me over, my father said that I was in bad shape, but he had seen much worse. Everyone, he observed calmly, went through it. He looked at me curiously, lowering his eyes behind his glasses. I thought that this was a gesture of consolatory wisdom, but I am now in my early sixties, and I think that he was focusing on me through his bifocals as he reflected to himself. If I did nothing long enough, my problem would go away, he said dryly. I had no idea what he was talking about. One afternoon as she prepared dinner in the kitchen, my mother observed that I had just graduated from Yale with honors in English. Surely, she argued, I should be able to write a book. Why did I not write a book?

Les Wolf had begun to drift that summer too. I had visited him at the small house he shared with a friend out in western Massachusetts. By his senior year, he and his roommate had named their little cottage "the ashram" and adopted a diet that consisted, as far as I could make out, of yogurt and preserves bought from the nearby farmers. He was deeply involved with a girl I never saw. Occasionally he would drive me to New Haven in his large blue Volvo, an incredibly lavish graduation present at a time when wealth was not flaunted on campus. Les had taken his senior year and the following summer off to study film in Sweden. "He will have a good time," said my now elderly pediatrician, Dr. Saunders. After graduate school, Les would get an MFA from the University of California at Irvine's distinguished writing program. He would work with the poet Charles Wright there and get an excellent job teaching creative writing at University of Redlands.

During the summer after we graduated in 1972, however, Les began to show signs of disturbance. He quarreled with this father. He tried selling floor cleaner door to door and made a killing at his father's apartment building. "What do you mean, not buy from the boss's kid?" the janitor at Sherri Park, where I worked, said.

In the midst of my crisis I called Dr. Saunders. My parents had known him since they lived in Glenville. They too had called on him when they found themselves in crisis. They had taken me as an infant to him when my doctor in Glenville gave me antibiotics. Looking into my mouth, Dr. Saunders quickly saw that I did not need antibiotics and thereby won their trust for nearly forty-five years. An avuncular, gruff, broad-shouldered man, he liked to boast about the wealth and success that his Jewish clients had achieved in Cleveland's postwar years. But now he thought of nothing but his young charges' future. He played tennis at the courts of my prep school, where he had known all my Jewish classmates and their parents. That summer, he was apparently seeing a number of students my age begin to drift, and he was more than a little angry with me. His knowledge of this dissolution weighed him down and seemed to make him, to my mind, a little sad. He had directed many of his patients to therapy that summer. He thus knew a great deal about the local psychiatrists and recommended one to me.

This therapist was a tall, sharp, very ironic Jewish man in his late forties or early fifties. Most of the young psychiatry residents I had encountered in therapy at Yale were formless. Dr. Frumkin knew the dance of therapy very well; he was form itself. He wore a white medical coat but did not seem pretentious. His first insight was that I had stopped working out of laziness, and he raised his voice at me when I almost went through the wrong door. It was the kind of tone a Latvian immigrant shopkeeper in Glenville might take with shift-less black help. I held it against him as class vulgarity, and he seemed to sense my disapproval. His time in this matter, my bad humor seemed to indicate to him, might be brief. This amused him a little, and he did not hold my rude-ness against me. In between a stream of clinical metaphors borrowed from the tradition of psychoanalysis, he spoke the language of Old World wisdom. "You are," he said, "under the calm exterior a smoldering volcano." At this point he paused for effect. He apparently knew something about my background. "You have an old Jewish problem," he said. "An aggressive, ambitious mother and a patient, satisfied father. Do not be too hard on your father; he has done well for himself." He smiled.

He gave me the first pills I ever took. Now in my sixties, I am a veteran be-cause of these pills and a lay expert on the doctors who dispense them. He may have been the best. I felt like a million dollars, suffused with sexual potential, and started asking out girls I hadn't seen in years. This pleased Dr. Frumkin to no end. Once afraid that I had offended one of my dates, I appealed to his judgment. In his best mode of Yiddish humor, he observed that a woman can run faster with her dress up than a man can with his pants down.

I had never taken drugs at all, and my prescribed medications seemed to open up the doors of perception to me. As soon as I came to my senses, as it were, I noticed that my parents no longer regretted the collapse of their old life in Cleveland and in the South. They were survivors and, like most people who escape a scene of horror, they spent their time joking about the terrors that had pursued them and failed. No longer did they see Cleveland as forming a coherent map; it was now no more than the shards and shreds into which the Negroes had torn the city. This had been funny, perhaps interesting for the city, and who knows what for the coloreds who had never leveraged significant power there. My parents had come to develop a subtle, paradoxical appreciation of extravagantly refurbished luxury cars, women on welfare dressed in high fashions, and wonton city violence in front of the storefronts where, as a young couple up from the South, they had bought collards and kale on Saturday mornings. In late middle age they were acquiring an ironic distance from the ghetto at about the same time the black arts movement rose to ascendency in the world of Afro-American culture. They still went to the West Side open-air market where I had seen my first carp—a huge bloodied gold fish eaten, my parents told me, by Hungarians and Polish people like the ones who supplied my father's school with coal and repaired the boilers.

My father tended to regard with humor the forms being taken by the soul of black folk. During the summer of my nervous collapse, he liked to tease me about the trends he was seeing. "When," he said, "will you begin wearing an afro and moustache?" And more mysteriously: "Do you know the fat woman who sits at the back of the bus?"

I did not answer.

"You know what I'm talking about," he said.

"I have," I said, "absolutely no conception of what you mean."

"The woman," he said.

"How do you know such a woman exists?" I responded.

This apparently upset him. He raised his voice. "Don't you worry about that," he said. "What I want you to do is to ask her for some peanuts."

I was stunned and could not speak for a few minutes. "How do you know that she has peanuts?" I asked weakly.

"They are," he said slowly and deliberately, "deep down in her purse. She will only get them out if she is forced."

The next Monday, in a state of partial recovery after a two-week absence, I went back to work. The manager had never had any trouble with me before, but now he seemed uneasy. He considered his position precarious. He had married into my friend's family and, the word was, he wished to move up quickly in the Wolfs' business. A short, slender, pale man, he wore horn-rims and olive-green poplin suits that betokened a kind of class aspiration that was untoward at Sherri Park. He was eager to do well and sensitive to the possibility of trouble.

One of the first things that I noticed in my new state of mind on the job was that many of the people around me did not work at all. I had not been aware that my supervisors who bossed me around stayed on their coffee breaks long after I left and toyed with two of the black maids, one a tall lithe woman in tight jeans and a revealing, partially open shirt. With their gold chains and expensive braided leather belts, they exuded the illicit luxury and eroticism—the purloined joie de vivre—of the city. I saw them coming out of empty apartments in pairs and individually. I ate lunch with the two maids and the janitors, one a tall gnarled man and the other a short grumpy fellow. The tall woman, I noticed, had a thick gold chain around her neck and wore a thin, but no less expensive, ankle bracelet. She had on a heavy perfume that smelled like floral spray. On her face were long scars that might in Africa have passed as ethnic markings; I surmised they were knife cuts. She was a recognizable character from my parents' dinner-table stories of inner-city Cleveland, and here she was at an apartment development in Beachwood. America was a complicated place. Across the table, the tall janitor reached down, obviously rubbing her hand against his member. Her skin was light, and she reddened a little. Afterward, she stared at him blandly. The tall man left. She sought out my foot with her toes and rubbed it tentatively. I looked in her face. She said something, but all I could make out was a hushed string of obscenities.

My observations of the other janitors changed my attitude toward work. I learned how to lengthen my time on the lawns, often hiding in a storeroom where the tractors and cutting equipment were stored. Adjacent to this room was a large closet in which the lifeguard kept equipment for the swimming pool. The two rooms were connected by a door that would not stay shut. After I had established a series of new routines, I noticed that the large storeroom never got warm and provided excellent shade from the sun. I spent a great deal of time there. Assorted refuse had accumulated on the floor, and I found a number of old high school yearbooks. It was refreshing to turn their glossy pages and look at the images of football players, cheerleaders, and newspaper editors from Beachwood High School. I knew the names of some of these kids from my Jewish friends at prep school. The kids in the photographs were clearly full of themselves in the way that upper-middle-class white high school students often are, but they did not look extremely bright. I thought smugly to myself that they deserved to go to Ohio State and Miami University.

I found an old copy of Erich Segal's *Love Story* and tried to imagine its owner, a freshman at Kent State imagining herself at Harvard. Of course, I had met such arrogant kids in New York City and New Haven. (The girls in particular disliked references to Cleveland, and perhaps these literary fantasies explained their obnoxiousness.) As I looked at the kids in the yearbook, who were obviously competing for the attention of their peers, their parents, and their teachers who wrote letters of recommendation, I sensed their absurd symptoms, and in some way, I began to sympathize with their teenage angst.

The black maid apparently changed her clothes there, for I found a few panties that still retained their organic feminine smell. I thought about her life: she probably had children and a boyfriend in the city who beat her. This little shed by the lawn surrounding the swimming pool in woodsy Beachwood was as much greenery as she would ever see. I surmised that she and the taller of the two janitors had trysted here. In my mind's eye I saw them: they collapsed on the ground, grunted, and went on with their lives as if they had just urinated, as Dr. Saunders might say. But, and this sad banality was very much to the point, that was probably all there was to the lives of most people.

I came across a yearbook in which the pictures of all the senior boys had been neatly and carefully annotated by the owner (I imagined it was a girl) and her friends in various colors. As far as I could judge, these girls were good students, probably obedient daughters. But on the pages were rasping expressions of rage and anger: labels such as "fucker," "cocksucker," and "asshole." The sentence-length commentary was much more descriptive. This banal quotidian world was, in the twinkling of an eye, illuminated by the psychotropic drugs dispensed to me by Dr. Frumkin. I had always been aroused by the smell of chlorine on a girl's skin, the tan lines on her thighs, the clean smell of hair rinse after she has showered. Across the hallway, the lifeguard pulled off her shift, revealing a black swimsuit. I sized her up. She was undoubtedly the daughter of an upper-class acquaintance of the Wolfs. She had probably been to Europe, and she wore bright-red Dutch wooden shoes that had probably been bought in Amsterdam; they would later become popular in New York. Her hair was knotted into a ponytail. A college student, she had barely lost her Fort Lauderdale tan from April. It immediately occurred to me that she was of a piece with the smiling girls in the yearbook, who I had earlier dismissed as beyond my notice. I returned to the pictures, hunching over to make out every word, only to have the slender black maid come up behind me and jog me hard in the ribs.

"You like white boys, don't you?" she said. "I thought so."

I could not speak.

She turned, getting ready to walk out.

"Fuck you," I said.

She said nothing in response and walked out. When I got home, my father asked me whether I had gotten any peanuts yet. I said nothing and went to my bedroom.

"Where are those goddamned peanuts?" he yelled up the stairs.

"You think you know everything!" I screamed, exasperated.

"I thought you would never learn," I heard him murmur in the living room.

The next day, the first person to confront me was the Ivy League–looking manager, red faced and sweating through his shirt sleeves. His fear had displaced his social aspirations; olive poplins and silk shirts were not made for his present state of mind. I was not, he informed me, to have lunch with the janitors and their female companions again. Nor was I to malinger in the pool toolroom. Only after some reflection did I realize that this made a certain kind of sense. I retired to the shed, where I read and reread *Love Story* and cataloged the Beachwood High School yearbooks in my mind.

Every morning the lifeguard came in to pull off her shift before she went to the swimming pool. She was very shapely and I enjoyed watching her. She took an increasingly long time as the days passed, making a point of not noticing me. Finally, after a week, she walked over to my side of the building and demanded to know why I spent all my time in there. I said nothing. No one, she observed, could figure out my place of origin.

As one grows up, one learns how difficult it really is to interrogate people. And it gradually occurred to me, sitting there, that I was dealing with a novice whose ineptitude was on a par with my own.

I said, "It's hot out on the lawn. I'm in here cooling off. Why don't you go outside and get on with your sunbathing?"

She reddened and walked out.

The next day, looking out the shed window, I saw her get out of her car, a late-model Camaro. On the back window she had a Miami University sticker. I watched her as she came in. She had obviously seen me watching her from the shed earlier, and she got angry.

"People say that you guys don't know what you want, but you do, don't you?"

I said nothing. She would have to fumble through this on her own, I had decided.

"Why don't you do any work?" she said, pulling off her jeans.

She had on a bikini today. The muscles in her stomach creased as she bent over. I said nothing. A little nonplussed, her tone shifted.

"I heard the other day that you went to Yale."

I was a little shocked, since I had never mentioned this to anyone on the job, and now on the defensive.

"Where did you hear that?" I asked.

"I was lying." She smirked and shook her ponytail. "All you guys go to Yale, and I wanted to see whether you were like everybody else."

She walked out.

That evening, I went straight to bed after getting home. I took two pills from my prescription bottle and watched the stars come out over our next-door neighbor's house. My generation may have been the last to experience prolonged longing as physical pain. Never had I been in such pain. Supine on my bed, I watched the ceiling spin. I had heard somewhere that lithium burns with a white flame, and indeed late at night, riding the high of my medication, I felt my manias refined into a soft metallic flame as I took in the darkness around me.

I returned to Sherri Park the next morning and took up the Beachwood yearbook again to look at the girls' swimming team. The night before I had imagined what the lifeguard had seen in me, a black boy in a khaki uniform riding a tractor. I did not look like a prospective graduate student at the University of Chicago. I looked like a kid from the inner city who, after a few scrapes, had lucked into a serious job that paid decently. She probably supposed that I knew the ropes of the city, its illicit joys, and its pleasurable hideaways. I was a good bet for a good time. I would, I decided, simply let my blackness work its magic tomorrow.

The next day I strolled into the shed; picked up a magazine; and, in defiance of the orders I'd been given, began reading, occasionally dozing off. As I read, I suddenly found myself unexpectedly covered with water. The lifeguard was there. She had poured a bucket of pool water over my head. I was completely soaked.

"I thought I would help you cool off," she said.

"You bitch," I said.

She tossed a pair of the maid's panties at me.

"Maybe you can change into these," she said, laughing.

She had a pretty smile. We were interrupted by the manager, who glared at both of us. He silently signaled her into the next room, where she put on her street clothes. I had not noticed that she wore a long, brightly colored muumuu. An hour later I saw her drove off. Never would I see her again. I sensed that we were at the point of reaching an understanding. It was too bad. Blacks and whites rarely understood each other on ideological terms. But real politics is the art of the possible, and I had just hit upon it. I had wanted to tell her that I admired her car and wondered whether she had gone to Miami to buy a decal and party in style, as so many of my Cleveland Heights neighbors did, and could she bring a decal to the pool tomorrow, as they were not sold in New Haven.

Nothing was said when I went to the office to pick up my final check, although the Wolf family never held my encounter with the lifeguard against me. Les's father even teased me about learning to swim. When I got home, my father listened to the story in satisfied silence. Weeks before, he had found a job for me at one of the university hospitals, near 105th and Wade Park, where he and my mother had lived when they first came to Cleveland. It did not seem like an unappealing prospect.

The hospital was a large building with a cavernous basement that I mopped and waxed by myself. The other maids and janitors flirted in the darkened classrooms and storerooms. On Friday nights I would go to the gravel-covered roof of the hospital and watch the ambulances bring the cut, the stabbed, and the shot into the emergency room. Downstairs one might see them triaged in lines along the halls. The young slender doctors were Jewish. They looked like the graduates of Beachwood High School, Kent State, Case Western Reserve, and Yale that they probably were. Their white smocks were covered with blood and other bodily fluids. They were getting their faces shoved in it. They were confronting life as it is. It was apparently quite a bit to take in.

They were residents and interns. I saw their half-filled paper cups of coffee on the floors of the large lecture halls. Their faces were grim. I was taking it in too. There was a toilet with a high window that looked out along Euclid. Coming in, I washed my face with fresh tap water. No one I ever noticed came in here, and I was completely alone. It was a little disturbing to notice how often I was alone. However, sitting by myself, I had, I was beginning to realize, heard and seen many strange things. Late at night, I smelled the breeze from the lake coming through the trees of Wade Park, over the lagoon, and into the hospital. It was fresh. I imagined my parents holding hands and walking through Glenville. At the house in Forest Hills some thirty years later, they are still larger than life to me as they bring in a carload of groceries each Saturday morning from the farmers' market just across the Cuyahoga River on the near West Side. With the money made from their rental houses in East Cleveland, they now traveled to Hawaii, where my father danced with hula girls, or Paris, where they rode a bus through the red-light district at night. But here in the darkened toilet, I imagined them recently having come to Cleveland in the early fifties.

I had spent the past four years reading literature, but I had not realized until then that my parents' life in the city was not unlike the romances I read in Spenser or Wordsworth, wish-fulfilling projections that attached themselves not only to a beloved but also to valued places and things. A city at its best evokes its citizens' political, social, and cultural possibilities. To see oneself and one's prospects in the city is to see one's being extended by civilization. Not to find oneself in the mirror of urban life is to experience the most profound alienation that modern society has to offer.

It is still remarkable to me that my parents extended their romance as young people in love to the romance of their expectations for urban life. They, however, as my mother liked to say, had made their lives, and I still had mine to make. And sitting, loitering in a hospital toilet, with the breeze from Lake Erie blowing in on a Saturday night, I realized that I had not even begun. I had, as far as I could tell, nothing but a few narratives, metaphors, and points of view—a set of odd stories, sly perceptions, and fuzzy memories. Thinking of my parents coming to Cleveland and working odd jobs in the Cleveland Transit System, Reliance Electric, and the sweatshops downtown, I realized that Darwin, who had probably heard it from his father, was right. I knew nothing. This knowledge, it now occurred to me, was more than I might imagine.